Literature:
the Book, the Place and the Pen
A Teaching Resource Book

By

Andrea Louise Ambler

and

Jerald Eugene Klocek

Illustrated by Christine J. Coates

Ambler Publishing Company
Pasadena, California

Literature: the Book, the Place and the Pen
A Teaching Resource Book

By Andrea L. Ambler and Jerald E. Klocek
Illustrated by Christine J. Coates

Ambler Publishing Company
1465 Pegfair Estates Drive
Pasadena, CA 91103-1909
(626) 365-1486
Info@AmblerPublishing.com
www.AmblerPublishing.com

ISBN Print Book: 978-1-7340456-0-4
ISBN E-Book: 978-1-7340456-1-1

Library of Congress Control Number: 2019950968

First Edition Revised. Printed in the United States of America

Revisions by One On One Book Production, West Hills, California

Dedications

This book is dedicated to the memory of
my parents
Dr. Wendell A. and Marion G. Morgan
to my late husband
Harold Leon Ambler
to my mentor and my late dear friend
Dr. Joanna V. McKenzie
and to my friend
Charles I. Hargrove

Andrea L. Ambler

This book is dedicated to the memory of
my parents
James E. and Mary L. Klocek
and to the memory of my mentor and dear friend
Margaret Mowrey Hamilton Moore

Jerald E. Klocek

It is with the reading of books the same as with looking at pictures;

one must, without doubt, without hesitations,

with assurance, admire what is beautiful.

Vincent Van Gogh

TABLE OF CONTENTS

Acknowledgments

We are grateful for the assistance and support of numerous people in completing this book: scholars, colleagues, friends and family members, and, most importantly, our former students.

Hayden Carney, DJ., graduate of Webb Institute of Naval Architecture with a B.S. Degree in Naval Architecture and Marine Engineering and a law degree from the University of Southern California. Hayden shared his vast knowledge and experience with copyright requirements and procedures.

Elliot Engel, Ph.D., scholar, author, college professor, leading authority on Charles Dickens and presenter of literary programs for children and adults. He earned his M.A. and Ph.D. as a Woodrow Wilson Fellow at UCLA. He reviewed the units on Shakespeare and Victorian literature offering valuable comments and suggestions.

Ralph Fletcher, graduate with B.A. degree from Dartmouth College and M.F.A. degree from Columbia University; teacher, poet, young adult novelist and author of children's books, and educational consultant. His professional books on what a writer needs aided us in developing our text.

Eleanor Ramrath Garner, graduate of Boston University, artist, author and editor. She wrote a compelling memoir of her experiences as a young American girl growing up in Hitler's Germany. Eleanor provided significant input on our memoir unit.

Charles I. Hargrove, graduate of California State University, Northridge; post graduate studies in Advanced Management at Harvard University. He is a friend who offered valuable suggestions, support and encouragement on the content as we developed our manuscript.

Paul Janeczko, graduate of St. Francis College in Maine and attended graduate school at John Carroll University in Ohio; teacher of high school English; prolific writer in poetry, novels, non-fiction and professional books and anthologies. Through his writing and personal connection, he was an inspiring resource.

Brian G. Morgan, graduate of Stanford University, Biblical scholar, teaching pastor and devotee of poetry. He is Andrea's brother, who offered poignant comments and insightful suggestions and a masterful analysis of Elizabeth Bishop's poem, "The Fish."

Eric Olson, DJ., graduate from Pomona College with a B.A. degree in history and a law degree from Harvard University. In addition, he was a teaching fellow at Stanford University. Eric offered advice, support and encouragement in the book's production and its distribution.

Gene Pepper, graduate of Stanford University, retired business consultant and author of *How to Save Your Business and Make It Grow in Tough Times* and *Memoir: The Stutterer Speaks*. He is a presenter of writing strategies and generously shared his ideas about writing a memoir and about the publishing process.

Fernando Pérez Hernández, graduate of National Polytechnic Institute, Mexico City, Mexico. He studied Communications and Electronics Engineering and worked as an electronics engineer. Having studied technical drawing, he provided the drawings for the coat of arms and the open book.

Silvia Maribel Pérez, graduate of the University of Mexico with a degree in computer technology. She served as an indispensable assistant to the authors, offering insightful and creative suggestions for formatting and in the actual formatting of the manuscript.

Fernando Pérez Reyes, graduate of National Polytechnic Institute, Mexico City, with a degree in computer science. He provided valuable input and support in the technical process of formatting the text.

Kostie R. Saba, graduate of California State Polytechnic University, Pomona, CA, with a degree in graphic design. He formatted the front and back covers of the book.

Phyllis Walker, graduate of University of Redlands, Redlands, California, with B.A. and M.A. degrees in English; post graduate studies toward a Ph.D. at UCLA; master teacher of English for middle school and high school, and curriculum developer for the Gifted Program with the Beverly Hills Unified School District. She offered poignant comments on the content of the manuscript, an editor extraordinaire.

Forewords

I am honored to write a foreword for this most remarkable literature textbook, lovingly created by Andrea Ambler and Jerald Klocek. Their passion for literature is fully on display in their preface which opens with the exclamatory "THIS IS IT!" and concludes with the enthusiastic "come in; come!" And when you, the reader, do indeed come inside this book, you will find that their excitement and zeal are downright contagious.

They wisely have organized their text by the four genres, those broad categories into which all writing falls: fiction, non-fiction, poetry, and drama. And, even wiser, they include a fifth--fairy and folktales--since this sub-genre contains the alluring and imaginative literature which we have all loved since childhood.

My favorite sections of this book are the "tasks" which were created to encourage student participation. I must quibble, though, with their terminology, since TASK means JOB, DUTY, or CHORE. These imaginative exercises are hardly such dreary burdens. No, they are actually all great FUN. There is a British term--a lark--which means "a delightfully amusing adventure." That definition is exactly what these "tasks" will become for the lucky students who engage in them. And since this book is chock-full of "larks," we need to call the combined exercises "an Exultation of Larks," since that is the poetic collective term used when describing many larks.

As you no doubt notice, my Foreword has become an Exultation (or High Praise) for Mrs. Ambler's and Mr. Klocek's outstanding text. Perhaps I'm a bit "forward" in my FOREWORD to be so enthusiastic in my praises, but, as I mentioned above, their joy in all things literary is dangerously contagious. I've clearly fallen victim to their Thrill Of The Quill, and I predict you too will come down with a raging reading fever as you peruse this delightful and invaluable book.

Elliot Engel, Ph. D.
English Professor
University of North Carolina
Chapel Hill, NC

Amazingly, the first sentence in the Preface states why the authors chose to write this book. They are, indeed, excellent teachers sharing their gifts and passion for teaching and learning. Much of the content in the book transported me back a number of years when I was an administrator in the Beverly Hills Unified School District and as an Associate Professor at Azusa Pacific University.

In this book, co-authors Andrea Ambler and Jerald Klocek masterfully address the teaching of various literature genres in a very practical yet detailed style. The reader is given background data regarding the author and/or text. The book is well researched so that if the reader wishes to delve deeper into a topic, an extensive bibliography can be found in some chapters. These authors know all aspects of the reading process and genres of literature. It is the reader's good fortune that they have delivered this knowledge in a very thorough and fun-filled manner.

Andrea Ambler and Jerald Klocek demonstrate that they are experts in curriculum content and instructional strategies to provide a quality literature program. Instructional ideas are presented with a variety of practice and hands-on activities to be used by students in collaborative groups or independently. Assessment is an essential item in their text. Assessment suggestions in different forms are included in each chapter.

It is an honor to recommend this book as I know it will become a treasured instructional resource book on many teachers' bookshelves. This book is truly a gift for all teacher of literature, regardless of grade level.

Beth Andersen-Perak, Ph.D.
Associate Professor, Emeritus
Azusa Pacific University
Azusa, California

Literature: the Book, the Place and the Pen is a much needed resource for any teacher of English or literature and can easily be adapted for use with both middle and high school students. The book explores the many genres of literature from fiction to poetry. It includes annotated reading lists with selections that will appeal to a wide range of students' backgrounds and interests.

The authors bring their decades of teaching experience to the book, providing detailed "how to" instructions for both teachers and students. They provide both content and context for teachers and specific activities for students that actively engage them in reading, responding to and writing about the literature they have encountered.

As a former principal and superintendent, I wish that I could have provided this resource to my teachers, especially those new teachers entering the classroom for the first time. From the first page, you sense the knowledge and passion for literature these consummate teachers shared with their students and now they are sharing it with all of you. Enjoy!

James W. Davis, President, The Davis Group, Ltd.
Author and Former La Canada High School Principal and Superintendent
La Canada Unified School District
La Canada Flintridge, California

This richly imbued text is a how-to book of the highest order. It will make about-to-retire and retired English teachers, like me, wish desperately that they had possessed such material early in their careers. It will, as well, earn the fervent appreciation of novice and mid-stride teachers, who will feel gratified to have discovered this exceedingly helpful material before their teaching journey winds to an end. It is a book written not by doctoral candidates or professional writers with little teaching experience but by veteran English teachers for other teachers, novice and experienced. In short, it is a book about teaching students to read and think about literature and then to write about it.

This book is both passionate and practical. Each of these outstanding teachers has enjoyed a lifelong passion for reading and a profound appreciation for fine writing; they wish to share those passions with others, students as well as teachers. The book is also practical, as all successful "how-to" texts must be. It offers teachers detailed information about every literary genre, followed by creative and meaningful tasks to challenge students. In addition, if offers numerous ideas for assessing student work. An example of the treasures that can be found between the covers of *Literature: the Book, the Place, and the Pen* is a list of Shakespearean Festivals in England and the United States. Also, a list of authors' homes or other places sacred to various famous writers is included, with pertinent factual information for each one.

Like the authors who, in their introduction, issued an invitation to the reader to enter their world of reading and response, I add my own adjuration:

Do come in! Come! And be delighted!

Phyllis Walker, Editor
Retired English Teacher
Beverly Hills Unified School District
Beverly Hills, California

There is no better way to learn how to write than to read, read, read. Great writing is not only personal but also has structure. Sentence structure, conflict, unique vocabulary, as well as creativity, all combine to create a great piece of literature.

This book is actually a pathway to writing through the study of literature. It emphasizes regular practice with complex texts, examines critical types of content, promotes text dependent questions, and provides a challenge for the students.

I can envision that it would be a guide for writers, teachers new to the teaching of English and literature, students, critics, and simply aficionados of the study of literature.

To begin, guide yourself through this book to grasp the wonderment of great writing and literature through to the end.

The book is structured so that anyone can read and grasp the fundamentals of any particular genre of literature. It is a guide; it is an outline; it is a handbook; it is a resource. Keep it on the shelf readily available to anyone who needs an extra push into the understanding and interpretation of a piece of literature.

"Books are the sepulchers of thought."
Henry Wadsworth Longfellow

Kathy (Longfellow) Cockerill
Retired English Teacher
La Canada Unified School District
La Canada Flintridge, California

About the Authors

Andrea Louise Ambler was born in Los Angeles, California and graduated from the University of Southern California, earning B.S. and M.S. degrees. She also attended UCSB, UCLA and the University of Hawaii.

Andrea has taught at the elementary through university levels. She began a teaching career with the Los Angeles Unified School District and then taught for the Department of Defense in Illesheim and Ludwigsburg, Germany. Later, she joined the Beverly Hills Unified School District, teaching middle school science, history and English. She also served as a University Mentor for the Department of Teacher Education, Azusa Pacific University.

She was the Apple Award recipient from the Beverly Hills Educational Foundation as "Teacher of the Year." In connection with the award, her principal wrote, "Andrea Ambler epitomizes the best that an educator can bring to a classroom. It is truly magical to see her interact with students…poetry, literature and drama come alive in her classroom. Students are transformed into historical and fictional characters, become authors of poetry books and interact with literature."

Among her activities were the development of a literature program for gifted and talented students (GATE), a state-supported program. In addition, she was appointed Language Arts Mentor Teacher for the teaching of writing in the middle schools of the Beverly Hills Unified School District. She served as chairperson for the district K-12 writing committee.

Andrea was a Fellow in the UCLA Writing Project. She made numerous presentations at state English conferences, conferences for gifted youth and the Chancellor's Conference at UCLA. Andrea was a consultant for McGraw-Hill Publishing Company in the development of *Distant Shore*, a text for a K-8 literature series. She was the co-author of *Keepers of the Flame: A Poetry and Prose Resource Book for Teachers*.

She has received the Outstanding Teacher Service Award from the Beverly Hills Chamber of Commerce, the Outstanding Teacher PTA Service Award from the Beverly Hills School District. She was awarded the Johns Hopkins University Teacher Recognition Award and has been listed in *Who's Who in American Education*.

Andrea lives with her husband, Charles Hardgrove in Pasadena, California, where they enjoy their resident toy French Poodle named Sophie Delamarre. Among her interest are reading, dancing. traveling, art history, opera and the theatre.

Jerald Eugene Klocek was born in Cleveland, Ohio, and graduated from Baldwin-Wallace College, now known as Baldwin-Wallace University, in Berea, Ohio, with a B.A. degree in English. He has also completed graduate studies at California State University, Los Angeles and Northridge; UCLA; UC Riverside, where he earned his M.A. in Curriculum and Supervision; and National University, where he earned an administrative credential.

Jerald has taught at both the middle school and high school levels. After completing one year of teaching in Ohio, Jerald moved to California to teach English at Monrovia High School, Monrovia; South Pasadena Junior High School, South Pasadena; and La Canada High School, La Canada Flintridge. Later, he taught at Valley Preparatory School, a private-independent school in Redlands, California, where he later served as Headmaster.

During his teaching career, Jerald has served in various capacities, including team leader, department chair and Coordinator of Attendance and Discipline. He was elected twice as President of the La Canada Teachers Association. He has served on many committees, including curriculum development, tobacco and drug prevention, Comprehensive Alcohol and Drug Prevention Education and Drug Free Schools, and the Southern California Teachers of English Conference Planning. He has been a workshop presenter at the "Centers of Excellence" at Southland Council of Teachers of English, the California Association of Teachers of English, and the College Board Advanced Placement Conferences.

Jerald is retired and now lives in the new city of Eastvale, California, where he enjoys active membership in his church, tutoring, traveling, working in his garden, caring for his two cats, Roscoe and Smokey, and reading in the shade of his covered patio.

About the Illustrator

 **Christine J. Coates** graduated from Otis College of Art and Design in Los Angeles. *Literature: the Book, the Place and the Pen* is her first book to illustrate. She works as an independent professional artist and muralist and has worked as a mural conservationist and assistant to Kent Twitchell at Nathan Zakheim and Associates in Los Angeles. She has painted numerous murals on buildings for clientele in Redlands, Riverside, San Bernardino, Yucaipa, Rialto, Palm Springs, Perris, and the Armand Hammer Museum in Los Angeles. Additionally, she has numerous private collections and exhibitions of her work throughout the Inland Empire and the Greater Los Angeles area.

Christine resides in Redlands, California, with her husband and daughter.

Preface

What we have loved
Others will love
And we will teach them how.
                William Wordsworth

THIS IS IT! This book is written for teachers by teachers to encourage the teaching of literature and responding to it. It is our fervent desire to share our knowledge and the lessons we have developed through our love of reading, re-reading and teaching literature, through our own education and our many years of combined teaching experience. Our goal is to encourage the beginning teacher and to reassure the experienced.

Good literature consists of works that reflect in some way the multi-faceted nature of life. As F. Scott Fitzgerald believed, "That is part of the beauty of literature. You discover that your longings are universal longings, that you're not lonely and isolated from anyone. You belong." Through literature, students learn to explore life and to consider options for themselves.

Our goal for students is to encourage them to become prolific readers in all genres – short story, novel, non-fiction, drama, poetry – to love reading and to become insightful thinkers and competent writers. Both teachers and students will be surprised, even delighted, by the discoveries they will experience from reading.

We believe good writing is evidence of clear thinking. Students should have many opportunities to write; and teachers should write, as well. We value inquiry, dialogue, and freedom of thought. We acknowledge high expectations for students.

Literature: the Book, the Place and the Pen addresses national language arts standards. It presents twelve chapters, each with ideas centered on various genres, together with tasks. Each chapter includes purposes and background information for teachers as well as inspirational and practical assignments for the students and concludes with assessments. The text also includes suggested book titles, many with annotations, and a bibliography for the chapters on Shakespeare and poetry.

The more that you read, the more things you will know.
The more that you learn, the more places you will go. . .

Oh, the places you'll go!
                Dr. Seuss

Come in! Come!

I could have never dreamt that there were
such goings-on in the world between the covers
of books, such sand storms and ice blasts of words.
Dylan Thomas, *Notes on the Art of Poetry*

Letter to the Teacher

Leading Students to Lifelong Literacy

Good teachers have a lifelong passion for learning and teaching and a goal to share these gifts with others. To accomplish this goal, they set and maintain high expectations of achievement for students and for themselves. They want students to become independent and responsible thinkers, with a love of reading and an appreciation for fine writing. Students need to learn the pleasures--aesthetic, intellectual and emotional--of reading and writing. Should we be asked, "Why teach literature?" we might reply, "We expose students to literary material so they will become more compassionate and recognize beauty. Of what value would it be to make a prosperous living unless one knows how to live well?"

The major goals of any classroom curriculum are to help students develop and improve their reading ability, speaking and writing skills and critical thinking. Research and common sense both tell us that the best way to achieve these goals is through **READING,** the process of engaging the text and connecting it to the reader's experiences. Yes, teachers want students to be dazzled by masterpieces, to love reading in the way that Norma Fox Mazer advocates, "The way we love ice cream is the way we should love reading. Passionate involvement, willingness to try all flavors, a lighting of the eyes, eating it in all seasons, a pint always in the freezer."

How Does This Happen? Work in a Print-rich Classroom

Very few students learn to love books on their own. Someone has to lure them into the fascinating world of the written word; someone has to show them the way. What a golden opportunity for parents and teachers to lead readers to the open door that lures them to one of life's greatest pleasures! Teachers need to make the classroom a place for ideas and to provide a variety of genre from novels, poetry, short stories, non-fiction and drama. All genres are valued, talked about, used and remembered. Students are encouraged to read daily (silently and aloud) and to understand that reading and writing are common behaviors both in and outside the classroom.

And now let us welcome the New Year
full of things that have never been.
Rainer Maria Rilke

WELCOME BACK TO SCHOOL

September, the month of new beginnings, has arrived. It is the time to look forward to the school year ahead and the journey within ourselves. A new chapter in your life is waiting to be written. New questions will be asked and answers will be discovered. I am delighted to be your teacher. I am eager to help you succeed this year.

As you read literary selections from various genre, you may, of course, choose and reject, agree and disagree with the authors' ideas. Yet, as you read their stories, your thoughts will surely expand, for they do what Emily Dickinson calls "joggle the mind" and expand the spirit toward wider horizons. This is a good thing in a world rushing so swiftly toward unlimited possibilities.

Reading, whether it is inside or outside the classroom, is an important part of the program. To assist you, book lists will be distributed, as needed. The lists will include high-interest book suggestions and works which are very challenging. Upon completion of the reading assignment, you will work on an oral and/or written task or project. The project will be evaluated as well as a performance assessment.

Fall Semester (Year)	**Spring Semester (Year)**
September	February
October	March
November	April
December	May
January	June

Student Signature: _____

Parent Signature: _____

Notes: Parent signatures are requested for elementary and middle school students to keep them on task and to inform parents of the assignments.

This program is based on a traditional school calendar…September to June. For other types of school calendars, modifications are necessary.

The Writing Process

How can I know what I think till I see what I say?
E.M Forester

1. Pre-writing
   - Brainstorming
   - Clustering
2. Drafting the first copy
3. Sharing/Responding
4. Revising
   - Add
   - Subtract
   - Rearrange
   - Substitute
5. Editing
   - Surface Correctness
     (grammar, punctuation and spelling)
6. Proofreading
7. Evaluating
8. Publishing
   - Display in classroom
   - School newspaper
   - Outside resources

The Revising Process

*I have rewritten - often several times -
every word I have ever published.*
Vladimir Nabokov

Content – Development – Organization

Addition
Add more specific details, descriptions, examples, facts

Subtraction
Delete unnecessary and irrelevant information, words, sentences

Substitution
Replace a word, a sentence or an idea with another to enhance clarity

Rearrangement
Move words, sentences or restructure sentences and/or paragraphs
to clarify ideas

The Editing Process

"Writing is like riding a bike. Once you gain momentum, the hills are easier. Editing, however, requires a motor and some horsepower."

Gina McKnight, The Blackberry Patch

STANDARD AMERICAN ENGLISH
Surface Correctness

- Grammar

- Spelling

- Capitalization

- Punctuation

- Margins

- Heading

- Consistent Format

Chapter 1

Through the Eyes of Others

Through the Eyes of Others

*I write all my... stories in a great surge
of delightful passion.*
Ray Bradbury

Genre: Fiction
The Short Story

To the Teacher
The number of days necessary to complete this project is the teacher's choice.

To the Student
Task One: Introduction

We read fiction to escape to unfamiliar times and unknown places; we read for the pleasure of recognizing familiar incidents; and we read to "joggle" our imaginations, making our lives richer. Although fiction comes from the author's imagination, it is often grounded in life experiences. As Virginia Woolf affirms, "Fiction is like a spider's web, attached ever so lightly perhaps, but still attached to life at four corners."

One type of fiction is the short story, a brief narrative. The modern American short story emerged with Edgar Allan Poe's tales of mystery and horror during the 19th Century. One of the pleasures of reading short stories is to appreciate the writer's craft and the techniques an author uses to create a written work. A short story can be both *concrete* (tells about incidents and actions) as well as *abstract* (reveals ideas, emotions and attitudes).

Reading a Short Story
Strategies

Reading short stories furnishes the mind with knowledge, but it takes a good reader to find meaning from the text. The reader must infer or make logical assumptions about the events and characters. Reading also requires the reader to question the word choice, the inclusion of facts and the omissions of others, then reflect on what the author is doing, how the author is doing it, and why.

The following suggestions are offered to help the reader understand and "get inside" the story:

- **Preview:** Question what is happening; search for reasons behind events and characters' actions.
- **Connect:** Make connections between what is read with what has been experienced, heard or read.
- **Predict:** Anticipate what will happen next and how the story might end.
- **Clarify:** Review and reflect occasionally on what has been read and decide if understandings have been altered.
- **Evaluate:** Form opinions and make judgments about the characters and events; probe for the central idea or underlying theme of the story.

Elements of the Short Story

Authors combine traditional elements of the short story to communicate their perceptions of the world.

1. **Length:** Is short enough to read in one setting.
2. **Plot:** Has one main plot, thus one main problem. Plot centers around problem and follows a pattern:
   Exposition: Introduces the story.
   Rising Action: Happens when the problem and complications are introduced.
   Climax: Occurs when the turning point is evident and the characters change. The conflict is resolved.
   Falling Action/Resolution: Comes at the end of the story and is also known as the *denouement,* a French word meaning "to unravel."
3. **Characters:** Includes very few people or animals.
4. **Setting:** Involves the time and place for the action of the story.
5. **Theme:** Focuses on the meaning of the story. It may be directly stated or implied. It is **NOT** the same as the subject of the story but is the author's central idea or insight into life.

The Author's Perspective

In addition to the elements of the short story, authors express different perspectives or points of view. The point of view is the view from which the reader hears, sees and feels the story. The most common points of view include *first person, omniscient third person* and *limited third person.*

- **First Person Point of View:** Through this point of view the **narrator is a character** in the story. This allows the reader to "see" the story through the narrator. The author uses the personal pronoun "I." An example is Edgar Allan Poe's "The Tell-Tale Heart."

- **Third Person Point of View:** Through this point of view the **narrator is** omniscient (all-knowing) and is **not a character** in the story but tells the events of the story through the eyes of **more than one of the characters.** The pronouns "he" and "she" are used to tell the story. Examples are Saki's "The Story-Teller" and James Ullman's "Top Man."

- **Third Person Limited:** Through this point of view the narrator **is NOT a character** but presents the story from the perspective of **one of the characters.** An example is Pearl Buck's "Christmas Day in the Morning."

Techniques Used by Authors

Authors apply various techniques to give unity to the plot and to keep their readers interested in the story. Suspense is created by including techniques such as "foreshadowing," "flashback" and "irony."

1. **Foreshadowing**
   As the "fore" in the word implies, the writer gives clues about events "before" they happen in the story. The authors Jack London in "To Build a Fire," James Hurst in "The Scarlet Ibis" and Richard Connell in "The Most Dangerous Game" made use of this technique.

2. **Flashback**
   Flashback occurs when the author inserts an interruption in the action of the story to present a scene that happened earlier. An example is Paul Annixter's "Last Cover."

3. Irony

Irony is the term given to literary techniques that show surprising, interesting or amusing contradictions. These include *Verbal Irony, Irony of Situation and Dramatic Irony.*

- **Verbal Irony** occurs when a character states one thing and means another.
  Example: When something bad happens, someone says, "Oh, that's great."

- **Irony of Situation** occurs when what happens is the opposite of what is expected.
  Example: A police station that was robbed or a fire station that was burned down.

- **Dramatic Irony** occurs when the reader knows more about the situation than the characters.
  Example: In Shakespeare's *Romeo and Juliet,* Romeo thinks that Juliet is dead and he kills himself. However, the audience knows that Juliet is still alive.

Through the Eyes of Others

Genre: Fiction
The Short Story
Task Two: Assessment for Point of View

Notes to the Teacher:
Having studied and discussed the short story genre, students are now ready to focus on one of the perspectives – *point of view*. This lesson is designed to focus on the *First Person Point of View.* Secure a copy of Sir Arthur Conan Doyle's "Adventures of the Speckled Band" or Daniel Keys' "Flowers for Algernon" or any other selection that focuses on **First Person Point of View.**

Day One
Read the story in class, either aloud or silently:
- Ask the students to identify the author's point of view.
- Ask students to offer support for their opinions with evidence from the text and to discuss them with the class.

Day Two
After the students have read the story and concluded that it was written from the *First Person Point of View*, they are ready to complete the assignment.

To assess student understanding of the concept, the following steps may be given verbally, written on the board, or reproduced:

Direct the students to place on their desks a sheet of blank white paper, a pencil, colored pencils or colored markers.

- Ask students to remove a shoe and sock. Suggestion: if students are right handed, ask them to remove the left shoe and sock; left handed, do the opposite.
  Also, if students appear uncomfortable in removing their shoes and socks to draw the outline of their foot, consider photocopying the drawing on the following page.
- Instruct students to place the paper on the seat of their desk or on a chair or on the floor and then draw an outline of their foot, using the pencil. Include details, such as toenails or any outstanding features.
- Inside the drawing, write a story from the *first person point of view* of your foot. Remember to use the personal pronoun "I". You are limited to the space within the outline of the foot.
- Use colored pencils or colored markers to embellish the design.
- Have students share their stories with a partner, in a small group or with the entire class and assess comprehension of the concept.

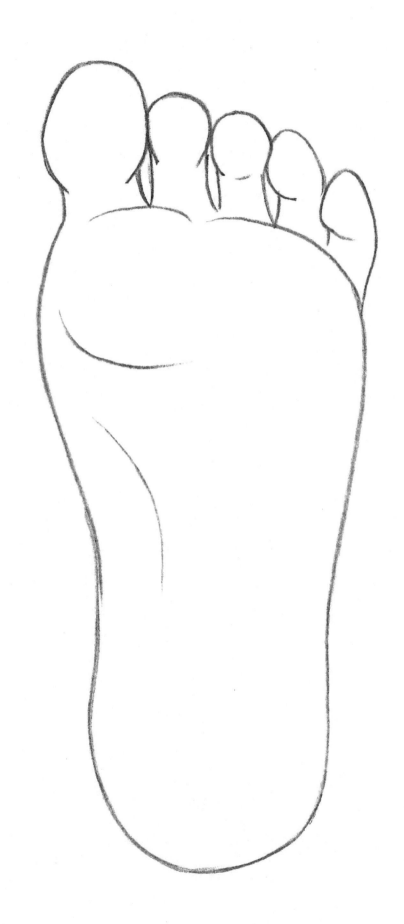

Through the Eyes of Others

Bradbury, Ray	The Drummer Boy of Shiloh
Dahl, Roald	Lamb to the Slaughter
	The Landlady
	Way Up to Heaven
Danziger, Paula	Remember Me to Harold Square (Selection)
Deal, Borden	Antaeus
de Maupassant, Guy	The Necklace
	A Piece of String
Doyle, Sir Arthur Conan	The Adventures of the Speckled Band
Ellis, Elizabeth	Flowers and Freckle Cream
Farley, Carol	Lost Now, Pay Later
Faulkner, William	A Rose for Emily
Finney, Jack	Contents of the Dead Man's Pockets
	The Third Level
Fitzgerald, F. Scott	Winter Dreams
Foley, Teresa	A Lesson in Discipline
Gardner, Mona	The Dinner Party
Gilbertson, Jean	If It Comes Back
Glaspell, Susan	A Jury of Her Peers
Godimer, Nadine	My First Two Woman
Hale, Edward Everett	The Man Without a Country
Hawthorne, Nathaniel	The Ambitious Guest
Hemingway, Ernest	A Day's Wait
	Soldier's Home
Hughes, Langston	Thank You M'am
Hurst, James	The Scarlet Ibis
Irving, Washington	The Legend of Sleepy Hollow
Jackson, Shirley	Charles
Jacobs, W.W.	The Monkey's Paw
Jimenez, Francisco	The Circuit
Kantor, MacKinlay	A Man Who Had No Eyes
Keyes, Daniel	Flowers for Algernon
Knowles, John	Phineas
Lardner, Ring	Haircut
Lawrence, D.H.	The Rocking Horse Winner
Lee, Cherylene	Hollywood and the Pits
Lessing, Doris	Through the Tunnel
Little, Jean	Who Are You (Internal Monologue)
Levoy, Myron	Aaron's Gift
London, Jack	To Build a Fire
Mansfield, Katherine	Her First Ball
Mazer, Norma Fox	Tuesday of the Other June
Mori, Toshio	Abalone, Abalone, Abalone
	Say It with Flowers
	The Loser

Nihei, Judith	Koden
Henry, O. *William Sydney Porter	After Twenty Years
	Gift of the Magi
	The Last Leaf
	The Ransom of Red Chief
	A Retrieved Reformation
Parker, Dorothy	The Last Waltz (Internal Monologue)
Poe, Edgar Allan	The Tell-Tale Heart
Rylant, Cynthia	A Crush
	Checkouts
	Stray
Saki * H.H. Munro	The Open Window
	The Story-Teller
Salinas, Marta	The Scholarship Jacket
Saroyan, William	The Hummingbird That Lived Through Winter
Sedillo, Juan A. A.	Gentleman of Rio en Medio
Singer, Isaac Bashevis	Zlateh the Goat
Sneve, Virginia Driving Hawk	The Medicine Bag
Soto, Gary	Broken Chain
	Seventh Grade
	The School Play
Stockton, Frank	The Lady or the Tiger
Tan, Amy	Two Kinds
Thomas, Piri	Amigo Brothers
Tolstoy, Leo	A Just Judge
Turgenev, Ivan	The Sparrow
Twain, Mark * Samuel Clemens	The Celebrated Jumping Frog
Ullman, James Ramsey	A Boy and a Man
	Top Man
Updike, John	Son
	My Father on the Verge of Disgrace
Vonnegut, Jr. Kurt	The Lie
	The Kid Nobody Could Handle
Walker, Donald	Rodeo Riders – A Special Breed
Wharton, Edith	Roman Fever
Wilson, Budge	Waiting

Through the Eyes of Others

Genre: Fiction
The Short Story: Reader's Log
Task Four: Responding to Literature

You have been on a literary odyssey. You studied the elements of the short story and strategies for reading this genre. You have learned about times past and present as well as familiar and unfamiliar cultures. These stories will now comprise a Reader's Log (portfolio), a means to assess your understanding of the craft of the short story writer.

Assignment

For **middle school** students, select **THREE** of the following tasks to complete. Select **ONE** question from Group I; select **ONE** question from Group II; select **ONE** question from Group III. **Be sure to select different short stories for your responses.**

For **high school** students, select **FIVE** of the following tasks to complete. Select **ONE** question from Group I; select **THREE** questions from Group II; select **ONE** question from Group III. **Be sure to select different short stories for your responses.**

Group I
1. Reflecting on the plot, what are the actions and incidents in the story? What ideas are expressed through the characters?
2. It has been said that the conflict is the essence of any story. Discuss a major conflict in the story and how it was resolved.
3. What role does the setting play in the story? Explain how it connects favorably or unfavorably to the plot.

Group II
1. Discuss how the characters' actions do or do not match their thoughts or words.
2. Discuss the point of view in one of your stories.
3. To create suspense, an author may employ the use of "foreshadowing" or "flashback". Discuss how **ONE** of these techniques was used in one of your stories.
4. Identify and discuss the author's use of irony: verbal, situation or dramatic.
5. Identify the author's central idea or theme toward the subject. What is yours?

Group III
1. Were you disappointed in any part of the story? Explain your reaction.
2. Discuss how the story offers insight into the human experience. Did you like the story? Why? If not, why not? Include supporting details from the text.

Assessment

Since students have been required to complete this major project, assessment is valuable feedback for the students. One suggestion includes a letter grade for content and another grade for mechanics, plus brief written comments by the teacher. However, the final decision for assessment is left to the discretion of the teacher.

Chapter 2

We are all booked up. . .

We are all booked up...

Outside of a dog a book is man's best friend.
Inside of a dog it's too dark to read.
Groucho Marx

Genre: Fiction
The Novel
Introduction

Reflecting on Groucho Marx's comic nature and his quote above, why is reading important? Why is reading a joy?

The best part of reading a book and even re-reading one that while the words remain the same, we change. Let's then begin with fiction because of its wide appeal. Within this genre, the writer skillfully tells the story and offers the reader a glimpse into another world. The author, John Updike, invites us to come to the writers' desks where "characters are spawned, plots are spun, imaginative distances are spanned." We may identify with the characters in the story; their experiences seem our own. The novels of Jane Austen, Charles Dickens and more contemporary authors, such as F. Scott Fitzgerald, Lois Lowry, J.K. Rowling and Gary Paulson, are an unfailing source of pleasure. Reading them takes us to other countries, other time periods and other worlds. Reading then provides a welcome escape from daily routine. We see the world from someone else's eyes, thus opening our minds to new possibilities. Keep Lincoln's words in mind: "A capacity and taste for reading gives access to whatever has already been discovered by others."

How Is the Novel Created?
Unveiling the Mystery

How does the author create a novel? First of all, a novel is fiction, primarily made up from the author's imagination. Just as an artist uses line, shading and color to create a painting, an author uses strategies of fiction to create a story. The strategies utilized include plot, character, setting, point of view, tone, mood and theme.

- **Plot** is the ordering of actions and events in a story.
- **Character**, usually a person, is a participant in the story.
- **Protagonist** is the main character.
- **Antagonist** is a character or force that opposes the protagonist.
- **Minor character** connects with other characters.
- **Setting** is the location and time of a story.
- **Point of View** is a literary device an author uses to focus on details, opinions or emotions.
    1. **First Person Point of View:** The narrator is a character in the story. The reader "sees" the story through the narrator. The writer uses the personal pronoun "I."
    2. **Third Person Point of View:** The narrator is omniscient (all knowing) and is not a character in the story but tells the events through the eyes of the characters. The pronouns "he" and "she" are used to tell the story.
    3. **Third Person Limited:** The narrator is **NOT** a character but relates the story from the **viewpoint of one or more of the characters.**

- **Tone/Mood** reflect the attitudes toward the subject and characters.
- **Theme** is the main idea or message of the story.

Books of Distinction

Book Awards

Recognition of excellence is given to authors who have written a distinguished novel, one that is original and creative. The categories for awards include authors who write novels for elementary, middle school or high school students. Numerous awards are offered. Below are some of the best known:

- **California Young Reader Medal** is a set of awards given for fiction books selected by California students. The categories include Primary (K-3), Intermediate (3-6), Middle School (6-9) and Young Adult (9-12).
- **Coretta Scott King (Author) Book Award** recognizes an African American author of outstanding books for young adults.
- **Eliot Rosewater Award** is chosen annually by high school students (grades 3-12) who live in Indiana. Eliot Rosewater is a recurring fictional character in Kurt Vonnegut's novels.
- **Michael L. Printz Award** is given for excellence in literature written for young adults.
- **Newbery Medal/Newbery Honor** is named for an 18th century publisher, John Newbery, who published books for children. In 1922, the American Library Association presented an award for the most prestigious book published the previous year. The award, named after the English publisher, has been given since that time. In 1971, the Newbery Honor Award was initiated.
- **William Allen White Book Award** is named for the renowned American newspaper editor, author and politician. The award is given annually and chosen by readers in grades 3-5 and grades 6-8 who live in Kansas.
- **William C. Morris Award** is given to honor a debut book published by a first-time author writing for young adults; finalists are also recognized.

We are all booked up...
Books of Distinction

Genre: Fiction
Task One: Reading a Novel

The great variety of themes found in novels makes it possible to draw pleasure from reading a book that matches your preference. You may select a novel to read from the "Book Award" list or a novel of your choice, whether it has suspense or mystery or one that appears to be completely imagined. Annotations have been prepared for **winners of the Newbery Award.**

Newbery Medal/Newbery Honor

Avi. *Crispin: The Cross of Lead.* This is an action-filled book set in 14th century England. A thirteen-year-old boy works the land for people who treat him with disdain. Accused of murder, he flees his village and eventually meets a juggler, Bear, who becomes his teacher and protector. His goal is to solve the mystery of his own identity and to fight the injustices of feudalism.

Avi. *The True Confessions of Charlotte Doyle.* In the 19th Century, a thirteen-year-old girl, Charlotte Doyle, is sailing from England to America to rejoin her family. She is the only female on the ship and experiences dangerous adventures during the crossing. The ship is manned by vicious crew members and a tyrannical captain. When Charlotte finally reunites with her family, she encounters further rejection and confronts another crisis in her life. How does she react? What change does she make in her life?

Cushman, Karen. *The Midwife's Apprentice.* The story takes place in Medieval England and focuses on the life of a homeless young girl called Brat. Jane, midwife, takes Brat as an apprentice. As the girl matures and gains confidence, she overcomes her difficult past and finds work at an inn. While at the inn, she meets a scholar, who is working on a book, and he introduces her to a new life.

Forbes, Esther. *Johnny Tremain.* The story centers around the themes of apprenticeship, sacrifice and conflicts between the Whigs, who want freedom from England, and the Tories, who remain loyal to England. Imagine living at the beginning of the American Revolution. The main character, fourteen-year-old Johnny Tremain, lives in Boston during this dangerous time. He works as an apprentice to a silversmith until his hand is badly burned.

Gaiman, Neil. *The Graveyard Book.* A child named Nobody, an assassin, a graveyard and the dead are the combination for a creepy, yet humorous tale. The child called Nobody is marked for death. He escapes and ends up in a graveyard. Who are his protectors?

Hesse, Karen. *Out of the Dust.* This is a powerful story set in Oklahoma during the time of Dust Bowl years of 1934-1935. The novel is written and the plot advanced through "free verse" poems. The main character, Billie Jo, lives through great physical and emotional struggles and develops courage in the face of adversity.

Hunt, Irene. *Across Five Aprils.* The novel captures the conflict among brothers during the American Civil War. The main character, Jethro Creighton, is the real grandfather of the author, Irene Hunt. Jethro lives on a farm in Illinois. As the plot unfolds, the war begins and Jethro's world is forever changed. His brothers, Bill, John and Tom, join the fight and he must struggle with the split among them. John and Tom side with the Union Army, but Bill joins the Confederacy.

Kadohata, Cynthia. *Kira-Kira.* Two sisters gaze at the stars and chant the Japanese word "kira-kira," which means "glittering." The reader easily sees from the beginning of the novel the love within this family. However, they face personal challenges and tragedy set against an oppressive social climate of the South during the 1950s and beginning 1960s.

Kelly, Eric P. *The Trumpeter of Krakow.* The novel is a dramatic tale of 15TH century Poland. The family of Joseph Charnetski must flee their home because of the invading Tartars and, in doing so, take the only treasure they manage to salvage – a family heirloom called the Great Tarnow Crystal. This priceless treasure is rumored to have magical powers to anyone who possesses it. Joseph's mission is to deliver the Crystal to the King before it ends up in the wrong hands.

Lowry, Lois. *Number the Stars.* During World War II, friends Annemarie Johansen and Ellen Rosen fear the German soldiers on the streets in Denmark. When the Jews are threatened, Annemarie's family hides Ellen and helps her family escape. The story is based on actual incidents and shows the values of courage and friendship.

Park, Linda Sue. *A Single Shard.* The setting of this novel is 15th century Korea, The main character, Tree-ear, is an orphan who lives under a bridge with his friend Crane-man. Tree-ear becomes intrigued with a nearby group of potters. Fascinated by their superb craftsmanship, he begins to assist the master potter named Min. Will Tree-ear demonstrate enough perseverance to overcome great hardship?

Paulsen, Gary. *The Hatchet.* Brian's parents are divorced when the story begins. Brian plans to visit his father in a remote part of Canada. As a parting gift, his mother gives him a hatchet. While traveling in a small plane, the pilot dies and the plane crashes. Brian lives and now must face survival, his only tool a hatchet.

Peck, Richard. *A Year Down Yonder.* Fifteen-year-old Mary Alice is living in Illinois during the Depression. She plans to leave Chicago to spend a year with her grandmother. She experiences initial apprehension in trying to adjust to life in a small community with a scheming relative.

Perkins, Lynne Rae. *Criss Cross.* The story involves the lives of four teenagers living in a small town, each character at a crossroad. They listen to the radio, wonder about the opposite sex and about themselves and come to understandings they didn't have before. They explore new ideas in their quest to find the meaning of love and life. Writing a third-person narrative, Perkins captures the incompleteness of adolescence.

Philbrick, Rodman. *The Most True Adventures of Homer P. Figg.* This is a poignant, eye-opening story centered on decisive moments in American history during the Civil War. Homer Figg must find and save his older brother, who has been illegally sold to the Union Army. During his journey, Homer encounters eccentric people.

Rylant, Cynthia. *Missing May.* Set in present-day West Virginia, Summer, an orphaned child has been passed from one apathetic relative to another. At age six, she meets for the first time her elderly Aunt May and Uncle Ob. Since Summer is ignored by her caretakers, Aunt May and Uncle Ob decide to take her to their rickety trailer home in the hills of the Appalachian Mountains. Summer thrives under their loving care.

Schlitz, Laura Amy. *Good Masters! Sweet Ladies!* Characters from a 13th century Medieval village in England spring to life. Monologues and dialogues reveal the characters and their relationships. The narrative offers humor, pathos and insight into the human condition and transports readers to a different time and place.

Spinelli, Jerry. *Maniac Magee.* Jeffrey Magee was orphaned when he was three and later leaves his uncaring relatives at age eight. "On his own, he runs for his life." The story imparts, as well, lessons about homelessness, poverty and qualities of tall tales.

Taylor, Mildred D. *Roll of Thunder, Hear My Cry.* The novel is set during the Great Depression in the Mississippi Delta. The story centers on the landowning Logan family as they struggle to survive in the face of attacks, illness and poverty. The characters reveal powerful messages.

We are all booked up...
Respond! Respond! Respond!

When you read a well-crafted novel, you encounter an intimate form of communication. You bring to the novel, or to anything you read, your own experiences of the world. Now that you have completed reading your book, you have an opportunity to respond through writing.

Genre: Fiction
Task Two: Writing the Academic Essay

This opportunity to respond through writing will take the form of an academic essay. Through this essay, you will show what you thought and what you understood about the novel. Academic writing is not "boring" but has a clear purpose. The goal is to convey ideas, descriptions or interpretations, while allowing you to include your own opinions. The tone is serious; take authority for your ideas. Elaborate with specific details.

- **Planning the Essay**
  Writing the essay involves planning, drafting, revising and editing the work. For this task, re-examine the elements of plot, character, setting and theme. Focus on what you want to say, then find support for your ideas from the text.
- **Guidelines for Writing**
  The following guidelines will assist you in the writing process:

Five-Paragraph Essay

Paragraph One: Introduction
Write a brief introduction of no more than three sentences. Identify the title of the novel and the author. Include a "hook" as an "attention-getter" so the reader wants to read your selection.
Examples:
- Use a quote from the text or another source.
- Begin with a startling statement.

Paragraph Two: Body Paragraph
Select either **Plot** or **Character**.
If you select **Plot**, choose **one** topic to answer:
- Identify and explain a major problem.
- Discuss the most exciting, disturbing or amusing incident in the novel.

If you select **Character**, choose **one** topic to answer:
- Discuss ways in which a character changed
- Which character did you appreciate? Support your opinion with details from the text.

Paragraph Three: Body Paragraph
Setting. Select **one** topic to answer:
- How does the setting contribute or enhance the plot and characters?

- In what way was the setting meaningful?

Paragraph Four: Body Paragraph
Theme: Select **one** topic to answer:
- What message or theme seems to hold the story together? Do not write a plot summary.
- Discuss how the author motivated you to see something in life from a new perspective.

Paragraph Five: Closing Paragraph
The final paragraph is brief --**three or four sentences.** It brings the essay to a close and includes your opinions.

Academic Essay

Assessment of Task: Five Paragraph Essay
Scoring Guide: Use a rubric score, opting for percentages or value numbers, or select another method, for example, letter grade.

Content/Organization

- **Introduction:** student identifies novel and author and includes a "hook".   _____
- **Plot:** student discusses a major problem or a touching incident   _____

OR

Character: student describes how a character changed or writes about a character he/she appreciated.   _____

- **Setting:** student describes clearly how the setting contributes to the plot and characters or how meaningful it was.   _____
- **Theme:** student elaborates on an idea that held the story together or on how the novel presented a new insight.   _____
- **Closing Paragraph:** essay is brought to a close and includes the student's opinion.   _____

Total Score   _____

Mechanics: Surface Correctness

- Correct grammar   _____
- Correct punctuation   _____
- Correct spelling   _____
- If handwritten, essay is legible   _____

Total Score   _____

Teacher's comments on the content, organization or mechanics.

Chapter 3

Something New…Something Extraordinary

Something New…Something Extraordinary

Read, read, read. Read everything…and see how they do it…
You'll absorb it. Then write.…

William Faulkner

Genre: Fiction
The Novel

The essential components for creating a novel include the following: plot, character, setting, point of view, tone, mood and theme. This assignment focuses on the element of setting.

Task One: Setting of a Novel
Introduction

With the writing of a great novel, the creating of a masterpiece, the author hopes to "write something new – something extraordinary." However, creativity, it turns out, isn't entirely up to the imagination. The setting contributes immensely to the story. Authors drew inspiration from specific places, including Mark Twain's idyllic Jackson's Island near Hannibal, Missouri; Louisa May Alcott's Concord, Massachusetts; Harper Lee's small town courthouse in Monroe, Alabama; Steven Spielberg's Pinnacle Peak Patio Steakhouse in Scottsdale, Arizona; and J.R. Tolkien's Middle Earth.

Authors write settings to serve specific purposes: to create a mood, to make the action seem more realistic, to contribute to a conflict in the story, or even to show the reader a different way of life.

In some stories the setting serves as a backdrop or context in which the characters interact. The setting then becomes crucial to the plot. An example is the description of the community in the novel *The Giver* by Lois Lowry.

Place and Time

In a novel, the setting is the place and time of the action. The place may be a specific country, region, community or home. The time includes not only an historical period --the past, present or future--but also the year, season, time of day and even the weather. Details such as customs, clothing and dialects also contribute to establish the setting.

Passages to Illustrate Settings

As you read these passages, notice the words the authors choose: precise nouns, thoughtful adjectives, colorful words, texture words and the sounds of the settings. These kinds of words make the paragraphs stand out as examples of masterful writing.

Where the Red Fern Grows by Wilson Rawls

"Our home was in a beautiful valley far back in the rugged Ozarks. The country was new and sparsely settled. The land we lived on was Cherokee land, allotted to my mother because of the Cherokee blood that flowed in her veins. It lay in a strip from the foothills of the mountains to the bank of the Illinois River in northeastern Oklahoma."

"In the spring the aromatic scent of wild flowers, redbuds, papaws and dogwoods, drifting on the wind currents, spread over the valley and around our home."

A Tree Grows in Brooklyn by Betty Smith

'Serene was a word you could put to Brooklyn, New York. *Especially* in the Summer of 1912."

"Late in the afternoon the sun slanted down in the mossy yard belonging to Francie Nolan's house, and warmed the worn wooden fence. Looking at the shafted sun, Francie had that same fine feeling that came when she recalled the poem they recited in school."

"The one tree in Francie's yard was neither a pine nor a hemlock. It had pointed leaves which grew along green switches which radiated from the bough and made a tree which looked like a lot of opened green umbrellas. Some people called it the Tree of Heaven."

The Call of the Wild by Jack London

"It was beautiful spring weather, but neither dogs nor humans were aware of it. Each day the sun rose earlier and set later. It was dawn by three in the morning, and twilight lingered till nine at night. The whole day was a blaze of sunshine. The ghostly winter silence had given way to the great spring murmur of awakening life. This murmur arose from the land, fraught with the joy of living."

"And amid all this bursting, rending, throbbing of awakening life, under the blazing sun and through the soft-sighing breezes, like wayfarer to death, staggered the two men, the woman, and the huskies."

To Kill A Mockingbird by Harper Lee

"Boo and I walked up the steps to the porch. His fingers found the front doorknob. He gently released my hand, opened the door, went inside, and shut the door behind him. I never saw him again."

"Neighbors bring food with death and flowers with sickness and little things in between. Boo was our neighbor. He gave us two soap dolls, a broken watch and chain, a pair of good-luck pennies, and our lives. But neighbors give in return. We never put back into the tree what we took out of it; we had given him nothing, and it made me sad."

"Atticus was right. One time he said you never really know a man until you stand in his shoes and walk around in them. Just standing on the Radley porch was enough."

Moby Dick by Herman Melville

"Call me Ishmael. Some years ago – never mind how long precisely – having little or no money in my purse, and nothing particular to interest me on shore, I thought I would sail about a little and see the watery part of the world…"

"There is nothing surprising in this. If they but knew it, almost all men in their degree, sometime or other, cherish very nearly the same feelings towards the ocean with me."

Lord of the Flies by William Golding

In the opening paragraph the author makes it clear that the setting is a tropical island.
"The beach was interrupted abruptly by the square motif of the landscape; a great platform of pink granite thrust up uncompromisingly through forest and terrace and sand and lagoon to

make a raised jetty four feet high. The top of this was covered with a thin layer of solid and coarse grass and shaded with young palm trees. There was not enough soil for them to grow to any height and when they reached perhaps twenty feet..."

Something New...Something Extraordinary

Reading is a great imagination booster. It helps develop a sense of creativity in you. When you are reading a novel, you imagine and may even experience something new.

Genre: Fiction
The Novel
Task Two: Reading a Novel

The following annotated booklist is a combination of elementary school, middle school and high school interest and reading levels. Select a novel to read from the list or one of your own preference.

Suggested Reading List

Caldwell, Bo. *The Distant Land of My Father.* The narrator, Anna, is a young girl living in the exotic world of prewar Shanghai, with her glamorous and young parents. Her father's great joy is sharing the city with his beloved daughter. When World War II begins, Anna and her mother leave Japanese-occupied Shanghai and return to Los Angeles. Her father remains behind.

Doer, Harriet. *Stones for Ibarra.* Two Americans, Richard and Sara Everton, are living in Mexico. They are the only foreigners in the town of Ibarra. They live among people who respect them but do not understand them. The reader sees the story through Sara's eyes: the disconnect between the two cultures--the inability to comprehend each other.

Golding, William. *Lord of the Flies.* William Golding was a Nobel Prize winner. His allegorical novel involves a plane that crashes on an isolated island. The only survivors are preadolescent British boys. Two boys, Ralph and another nicknamed "Piggy," attempt to establish order. The semblance of order quickly deteriorates with disastrous consequences.

Hailey, Elizabeth Forsythe. *A Woman of Independent Means.* The novel is written in letter form. The story is centered on the main character, Bess Seed Gardener, a loving, precocious, bossy, yet believable woman living in Texas during the early part of the 20th Century. The reader sees through the growth of Bess how she becomes a "woman of independent means."

Herzen, Lane von. *Copper Crown.* The author draws upon family stories passed down from her Texan grandmother and mother. She writes a novel about the forces of conflict and racial violence and about reconciliation and friendship. Two young women, Cass and Allie, one white and one black, decide to adventure out on their own in search of a better life.

Konigsburg, E. L. *The View from Saturday.* Four students, with their own individual stories, develop a bond and attract the attention of their teacher, Mrs. Olinski. She was returning to teaching after being severely injured in a car accident. This is a story about a team, a class, a school and a series of contests.

Lee, Harper. *To Kill a Mockingbird.* Scout and Jem Finch grow up in a rural town in Alabama during the Depression years. It is summer; and to amuse themselves, they try to entice a reclusive neighbor, Boo Radley, to come out of his house. Their father, Atticus, is a single parent, who tries to rear his children with love and respect for their individualism.

L'Engle, Madeleine. *A Wrinkle in Time.* This science fiction fantasy novel revolves around a young girl named Meg and her eccentric but brilliant brother, Charles. They share adventures as they travel through time and space to find and rescue their father, a scientist. Their father has been studying "tessering," a form of space and time travel, when he disappeared.

Levoy, Myron. *Alan and Naomi.* This story is set in New York after World War II. Urged by his parents, Alan agrees to help Naomi, the neighbor living upstairs. She came from war torn Europe and experienced memories of Nazi brutality. She now refuses to speak. Alan uses humor to break her silent world.

Lewis, C. S. *The Chronicles of Narnia.* This is a series of fantasy novels, the first of which is *The Lion, the Witch and the Wardrobe.* It tells of four children who leave London at the outbreak of World War II to stay in the English countryside. While staying with Professor Kirke, they discover a wardrobe that leads them to the world of Narnia.

London, Jack. *The Call of the Wild.* The main setting is the Yukon Territory during the years of the Klondike gold rush in the 1890s. London's descriptions are effective in writing not only of the harsh realities of this hostile environment but also of its unique beauty. The story centers on a dog named Buck, which is a cross between a St. Bernard and a Scottish shepherd. Buck, taken from his home in the Santa Clara Valley in California, must survive the rigors of the frigid North and the cruelty of his captors.

Lowry, Lois. *The Giver.* The setting of *The Giver* is a utopian world where there is no war, pain, color, few choices and little emotion. Everything is pleasant. Gradually, the society becomes dystopian. The story follows a boy named Jonas through the twelfth year of his life. He faces a dilemma: should he remain with the community in a safe but sheltered life or should he escape in pursuit of a life full of color, choices and love, but potentially dangerous?

Melville, Herman. *Moby Dick.* The narrative tells the adventures of a sailor, Ishmael, and his voyage on the whale ship *Pequod* under the command of Captain Ahab. Ishmael learns that the captain has one goal in mind: to find Moby Dick, a ferocious white sperm whale, and to seek revenge against the whale, which had snapped off the captain's leg.

Peck, Robert Newton. *A Day No Pigs Would Die.* This novel is set in Vermont during the 1920s and evokes both the harshness and compassion of Shaker customs. Twelve-year-old Robert is given a newborn pig by a grateful neighbor. He names the pig Pinky and it becomes his beloved pet. Robert eventually is faced with the difficult task of helping his father kill Pinky.

Rawls, Wilson. *Where the Red Fern Grows.* The novel is set in the hills and river bottoms of the Ozark Mountains in eastern Oklahoma. The land is ideal for farming and the wooded areas support animals--deer, opossums, raccoons and an occasional mountain lion. Billy, the protagonist in the story, is filled with "puppy love." He dreams about having a dog, specifically a coonhound. Billy, full of determination, works hard to realize his dream.

Rowling, J. K. *Harry Potter and the Philosopher's Stone.* When Harry was an infant, his parents were killed by an evil wizard known as Lord Voldemort. Even though Harry survived, he became a lonely, miserable young boy. At age eleven, his world is turned upside down when he learns that he is actually a young wizard.

See, Lisa. *Snow Flower and the Secret Fan.* The novel takes place in 19th Century China. In a remote community, a young girl named Lily, at the age of seven, is paired with another young girl named Snow Flower. Snow Flower introduces herself to Lily by sending her a silk fan. Their friendship lasts a lifetime. Both girls experience the cruel custom of foot binding. They reflect on this agony, their arranged marriages and their shared loneliness.

Smith, Betty. *A Tree Grows in Brooklyn.* The story focuses on an Irish-American family living in Brooklyn, New York, at the beginning of the 20th Century. Francie Nolan lives in a tenement neighborhood with her young brother, Neeley, and their parents, Johnny and Katie. Francie relies on her love of reading and her imagination in order to escape the impact of the family's poverty.

Steinbeck, John. *Of Mice and Men.* The setting is California during the Great Depression of the 1930s. This novella tells the story of George Milton and Lennie Small, two migrant ranch workers. They move from place to place in search of better job opportunities and their shared dream to own land and their own ranch. The dream is destroyed when they face a menacing situation.

Taylor, Theodore. *The Cay.* When World War II begins, twelve-year-old Phillip and his mother board a ship for Virginia. It is unsafe for them to remain in Curacao. The ship is torpedoed; Phillip is blinded and stranded on an island with a black man named Timothy and a black cat named Stew Cat.

Traven, B. *The Treasure of the Sierra Madre.* By the 1920s, the violence of the Mexican Revolution had subsided. The setting for the novel takes place at this time. Down-and-out Americans meet in the city of Tampico and discuss how to change their financial distress. They set out to discover gold in the remote Sierra Madre Mountains. In the process, they encounter bandits.

Yep, Lawrence. *Dragonwings.* This novel depicts the Chinese community of the early 1900s and the challenges they faced as immigrants living in San Francisco. Moon Shadow comes to America to be with his father, Windrider. They learn about the Wright brothers' flying machine and dream that they can build a better one.

Zindell, Paul. *The Pigman.* Two lonely high school students, John and Lorraine, find one another and Mr. Pignati, whom they rename "The Pigman." Their energy, laughter and love do not last when a cruel joke is played on "The Pigman."

Something New...Something Extraordinary
Settings

Genre: Fiction
The Novel
Task Three: Responding to the Settings

You have read a novel. Now, you are asked to select and record three passages from the novel describing three different settings. Give the title of the book, the author and the page number for each. Copy carefully each passage for the settings you selected. Below each passage write a brief paragraph commenting on the following:

- How does each setting connect with the plot?
- How does the setting help you visualize the place and time?
- Why is each setting meaningful?

Support your comments with evidence from the text.

Something New...Something Extraordinary
Settings

Assessment

In evaluating this assignment, a holistic approach is one option.

To earn a grade of "A" the student has completed all of the following:

- Includes three samples of settings.
- Includes reactions to each passage and its significance.
- Supports comments with details from the text.

A grade of B, C or D indicate that the final product is not as fully developed.

Note to the Teacher

It is suggested that comments on the content be made as well as comments on the surface correctness of the writing.

- Grammar
- Punctuation
- Spelling

Something New...Something Extraordinary

Genre: Fiction
The Novel
Task Four: Creating Your Own Setting

You have studied the significance of the setting in a novel. You have read passages from authors that represent masterpieces of writing. Furthermore, you have read a novel and selected passages that represented examples of well-crafted descriptions. Reflecting on William Faulkner's quote, "Read, read, read. Read everything...and see how they do it...You'll absorb it. Then write...," your task now is to "write" by describing a setting -- the classroom.

Procedure:
Our classroom offers a springboard for writing about setting. This setting also includes people. As you sit quietly at your desk, carefully observe your surroundings. Take mental note of your impressions: images, colors, shapes, sounds, smells and textures.

- As a quick write, for the next ten to fifteen minutes jot down, non-stop, your observations of the classroom, using words, phrases and sentences. Write what you see in reality and/or from your imagination.

- Review your notes and highlight those observations that are important to you.

- Compose a draft that reflects your perception of the classroom's setting. Include carefully selected details that support your statements.

- Finalize this writing at home for the next few days and bring the final draft to class on the designated day.

- The assessment of this assignment will be done by pre-selected adult judges. In place of your heading, **select a four digit code number** and place it in the upper right hand corner of your paper.

Something New...Something Extraordinary

Assessment

Writing Awards and Pizza Party

- On the designated due date, the papers will be collected and assessed by a panel of pre-selected adult judges.
- The judges will be asked to select the top three papers for a first, second and third prize.
- After the judges have read, discussed and selected the three top papers, the teacher will arrange a classroom pizza party, at a time convenient for the judges.
- The judges will announce the winners and present the awards-- a certificate, a trophy, etc.
- The winners are encouraged to share what they wrote.

Further assessment is left to the discretion of the teacher.

Chapter 4

Catching Sight of the Past

Catching Sight of the Past

I easily sink into mere absorption of what other minds have done,
and should like a whole life for that alone.

George Eliot (1884)

Genre: Fiction
The Novel: Historical Fiction
Introduction

Historical Fiction presents a story set in the past during a notable period or events in history and generally includes actual historical persons. However, the main characters tend to be fictional. Moreover, authors attempt to capture the details regarding manners, political events and social customs of the era.

Whether the authors' focus on the Medieval Crusades, the early American Revolutionary War or events in the early 21st Century, they aspire to "catch the reader" from the beginning of the storyline and to keep the reader turning pages. They are challenged to create interesting, believable plots, outstanding characters and strong themes.

Since this is historical fiction, "artistic license" is permitted in how the subject is presented. Simply put, "artistic license" means that a writer is given leeway in his or her interpretation of the actual historical period or events. "Artistic license" sometimes results in controversy because of the writer's interpretation of held beliefs. Writers, however, are allowed to take liberties with the facts in order to craft a good story.

Catching Sight of the Past

Genre: Fiction
Historical Fiction
Task One: Reading a Novel

The following annotated booklist is a combination of elementary school, middle school and high school interest and reading levels. Select a novel from the list provided or one of your own choosing.

Buck, Pearl. *The Good Earth.* This novel chronicles the social and political upheaval in China during the 1930's. Wang Lung's life is told from the beginning of his manhood and his acquisition of a wife to his last days. He works his way to become rich and important, as he struggles to give his sons a good life.

Collie, Lincoln and Collier, Christopher. *My Brother Sam Is Dead.* Tim, a young boy, grows up during the turbulent time of the American Revolution. His brother, Sam, returns home from Yale to join the Continental Army to fight the British. His father is outraged since he is a loyal supporter of the King. The novel integrates the nature of the American Revolution and a family with mixed loyalties.

Crane, Stephen. *The Red Badge of Courage.* Set during the American Civil War, Henry Fleming, a young naïve man, is eager to experience the glory of war. However, he soon faces the truth about war and his own self-identify on the battlefield. As the first encounter with the enemy approaches, Henry wonders if he will be brave in the face of battle. Panicking and fleeing during an early battle, Henry begins a journey of self-discovery as he struggles with his conscience and re-examines his opinions about war, friendship, courage and life.

Cullen, Lynn. *I Am Rembrandt's Daughter.* The novel is told through a series of flashbacks describing main incidents in Cornelia's childhood and teenage life. She is the assumed daughter of Rembrandt van Rijn, the artist who works in poverty. From 17th century social customs to the thrill of romance, Cornelia tells her tale of family drama along the banks of Amsterdam's famous canals.

Cushman, Karen. *Catherine Called Birdy.* Fourteen-year-old Catherine reveals through her diary a portrait of life during the Middles Ages. Catherine feels trapped. Her mother tries to make her into a fine lady, accomplished yet docile. Her father conspires to marry her off to a rich man, regardless of how awful it might be for her. Through wit and trickery, Cassie attempts to rid herself of undesirable suitors.

Cushman, Karen. T*he Midwife's Apprentice.* The novel tells of a homeless girl called Brat, living during the Middle Ages. She sleeps on a dung heap. She meets a midwife and is able to convince this midwife to allow her to work for food. Eventually, she becomes an apprentice and learns to hope for a better future.

Dickens, Charles. *A Tale of Two Cities.* The novel depicts the plight of the French peasantry, the brutality of the revolutionaries and the political corruption in the early years of the revolution. The main characters are Charles Darnay, a former French aristocrat and victim of the revolution, and Sidney Carton, an English barrister, both of whom fall in love with Lucie Manette. Intrigue, the desire for revenge and the secret of Madame Defarge's knitting lead Sidney Carton to the guillotine. The novel closes with one of the most quoted lines from a literary masterpiece.

Dumas, Alexander. *Man in the Iron Mask.* During the French Revolution, a young prisoner has languished for eight years deep in the Bastille, his face hidden from all. He does not know his true identify nor the crime that sentenced him there. Aramis, one of the original three musketeers, bribes his way into the Bastille to reveal a shocking truth to the prisoner. This revelation could topple King Louis XIV of France from his throne.

Fitzgerald, F. Scott. *The Great Gatsby.* In this novel, F. Scott Fitzgerald chronicles in a snapshot the 1920s Jazz Age. Through one of the main characters, Jay Gatsby, we witness and experience the super-glamorous world of the wealthy and the accompanying emptiness of their morally decadent world. Driven by his pursuit of passion as the expense of all else, Jay Gatsby is led to his own ultimate destruction.

Fleischman, Paul. *Bull Run.* By 1861, the beliefs of a divided nation are on a path to war. On July 21, the first shot is fired and the Civil War's first battle, known as Bull Run, begins. Through this story the reader comes to know 16 characters from different backgrounds (Northern and Southern) and learns of their ideas and experiences as well as the brutal consequences of war.

Fowles, John. *The French Lieutenant's Woman.* Charles Smithson is a 19th century Victorian gentleman, who is engaged, becomes fascinated by a beautiful woman named Sarah Woodruff, who is standing on a breakwater and staring out to sea. Wanting to help Sarah, he falls deeply into her secrets and mystery. Though Charles is both protagonist and antagonist as we see things mostly from his point of view, Sarah is the center of the narrative. Delving into the subjects of meditation, authentic existence, evolution, Marxism, this Victorian love story has three different endings.

Geras, Adele. *Troy.* This is a retelling of the Trojan War. Paris swept Helen away from her husband in Greece to his home in Troy. This incident caused a war between the Trojans and the Greeks. Paris and Helen must live inside a walled city, where food is scarce and death is common. After ten years of war, the Greeks present a giant wooden horse as a peace offering. Unfortunately for the Trojans, the horse proves to be their downfall.

Greene, Bette. *Summer of My German Soldier.* Patty, a twelve-year-old Jewish girl from Arkansas, meets Anton, a German World War II POW. Anton, whom she hides above her father's garage, helps her realize during their growing friendship that she is a person of value.

Hemingway, Ernest. *A Farewell to Arms.* Set in Europe during WW I, a young American student volunteers to serve in the Italian army. He is wounded and sent to a hospital in Milan where he falls in love with an English nurse. After his recovery, he returns to the front but deserts and travels to Switzerland with his young wife to start of new life. There, they experience another tragedy and are unable to live a happy life.

Hemphill, Stephanie. *Wicked Girls: A Novel of the Salem Witch Trials.* Told in verse, this story narrates a portrait of the Salem witch trials. It is revealed from the perspective of three young girls living in the community in 1692. What starts out as a game becomes a witch hunt. One character, Ann Putnam puts in motion a chain of events that change the lives of people around her.

Hesse, Karen. *Letters from Rifka.* This is the story of a young girl, Rifka, and her family who escape from the *programs* (unprovoked attacks) of 1919 Russia. The plot is revealed through a series of letters from Rifka to her cousin Tovah, who is still in Russia. Rifka's family arrive in Antwerp, Belgium and face yet another crisis.

Hesse, Karen. *Stowaway.* Nicholas, an 18th century stowaway, boards a ship in an attempt to escape the life he hates in London. It is the summer of 1768, and he is an eleven-year-old butcher's apprentice when he climbs aboard the ship. Once aboard, he learns that the captain and crew are on a secret mission. During his three-year voyage, he encounters many challenges.

Ho, Minfong. *The Clay Marble.* Dara, her mother and her older brother are fleeing war-torn Cambodia in 1980. They seek shelter in a refugee settlement near the Thailand border. Dara's need to belong is met in unexpected ways.

Hugo, Victor. *The Hunchback of Notre-Dame.* In the Gothic towers of the Notre-Dame Cathedral lives Quasimodo, the hunchbacked bell ringer. Mocked and shunned for his appearance, he is pitied by Esmeralda, a gypsy dancer. When Esmeralda rejects the approaches of the sinister, lecherous Archdeacon Claude Frollo, he plots to destroy her. Only Quasimodo can save her.

Jackson, Dave. *Spy for the Night Riders: Martin Luther.* Seeking an education, fifteen-year-old Karl Schumacher travels to Wittenberg, German in 1520. There, he becomes a servant to the university professor, Dr. Martin Luther. Luther tutors Karl in exchange for his labor. When a poster on the church door declares Luther a heretic, Karl travels with Luther to appear before the emperor's Imperial Council in the city of Worms. Will his life be in danger as well as Luther's? Who are the "night riders"? Who can Karl trust?

Levitin, Sonia. *Journey to America.* In 1938, Jews were living in great fear in Germany. Lisa's father escapes to America, promising to send for Lisa, her mother and two sisters. Until then, they are to live in Switzerland. While there, they experienced hardships that none of them ever could have ever imagined.

Mead, Alice. *Girl of Kosovo.* The novel is based on the experiences of an Albanian family living in Kosovo. It tells the story through the eyes of a young eleven-year-old girl named Zana. The Albanians have been denied basic freedoms, and relationships with Serbs are strained. Zana worries about their home, the farm and her family. Her worst nightmare is realized when the village is bombed.

Meyer, Carolyn. *Loving Will Shakespeare.* This novel brings the reader into the essence of life and love in a country village during the Elizabethan era. Anne Hathaway's life has been intertwined with William Shakespeare's since his birth. Their families connect and Ann and William become friends. Years later their feelings go beyond friendship.

Meyer, Carolyn. *Mary, Bloody Mary.* This is a fictionalized account of the childhood and history of Mary Tudor, who was the daughter of Henry VIII and the first Queen Catherine. Mary's childhood is a classic tale of a young princess who is heir to the throne of England. As the story unfolds, it explores the intrigue of the dramatic rule of her father, his affair and his marriage to Anne Boleyn. Mary faces dire consequences and struggles against forces beyond her control.

O'Dell, Scott. *Streams to the River, River to the Sea.* The story opens with the kidnapping of the Shoshone Indian princess, Sacagawea. Her peaceful existence is shattered; however, she faces her situation with a cruel husband with dignity. She experiences joy and sorrow when she joins the Lewis and Clark expedition, trailblazing a path to the Pacific.

Ostlere, Cathy. *Karma: A Novel in Verse.* The year is 1984, and fifteen-year-old Maya and her father are headed for India. They take with them the ashes of her mother, who has committed suicide. They arrive in Delhi on the eve of the assassination of Prime Minister Indira Gandhi who is gunned down by Sikh bodyguards and whose murder causes chaos and riots in Delhi. Sadly, Maya becomes separated from her father.

Remarque, Erich Maria. *All Quiet on the Western Front.* Paul Baumer enlists with his classmates in the German Army during World War I. Youthful and enthusiastic, they become soldiers. Despite what they have learned as soldiers, they collapse under the first bombardment. As the war continues, Paul adheres to a single vow: to fight against the principles of hate that pits young men of the same generation but different uniforms against each other — if only he can survive.

Richter, Conrad. *The Light in the Forest.* The novel, an American classic, is a sensitively told story of a white boy brought up by Indians. When John Butler was a child, he was taken from his parents in Pennsylvania by the Lenni Lenape Indian tribe of Ohio. He then was adopted by the great Indian warrior Cuyloga and re-named True Son. John eventually thinks of himself as Indian.

However, 11 years later, his tribe signs a peace treaty and a provision states that all captives must be returned, including fifteen-year-old John. He returns to a forgotten family, as well as strange customs.

Rinaldi, Ann. *A Break with Charity: A Story About the Salem Witch Trials.* This is an enthralling, authentic story centered in the dark period of America's past -- the Salem witch trials of the 17th century. Several young girls spread malicious lies, which result in false confessions from helpless victims.

Rinaldi, Ann. *In My Father's House.* The story is set during the Civil War and is based on events in the lives of the McLean family. The war begins on Wilmer McLean's property at Manassas. It ends hundreds of miles away, where he has moved to his new home at Appomattox Court House. Included in the novel are historical battles, resentment against profiteers and the signing of the peace agreement.

Rinaldi, Ann. *The Last Silk Dress.* Susan, a high-spirited, beautiful fourteen-year-old girl living during the Civil War, vows to do something meaningful to help the Confederacy. Against her mother's wishes, she and her friend Connie collect silk dresses from the rich ladies of Richmond. They plan to make a hot-air balloon to spy on the Yankees. However, the issues behind the war aren't as clear cut as Susan believes.

Rinaldi, Ann. *Wolf by the Ears.* Harriet Hemings is a young woman who lives at Monticello, Thomas Jefferson's home. Rumors are that Jefferson is her father, but her mother, Sally Hemings, a slave of the household, will not acknowledge the truth of this rumor. Facing a major dilemma, Harriet must decide whether to remain in this protected world or to choose freedom and leave her family behind.

Salisbury, Graham. *Under the Blood-Red Sun.* Hawaii is the setting for the novel where the main character, Tomi, lives. His grandfather and parents were born in Japan and immigrated to Hawaii to escape poverty. World War II seems far away to a young boy, who is busy playing ball with his team. When the Japanese attack Pearl Harbor, his father is interned; and Tom realizes how horrifying it is in these days to be Japanese.

Steinbeck, John. *Grapes of Wrath.* Set during the Great Depression, the novel focuses on the Joads, a poor family of sharecroppers. The Joads are driven from their home by drought, economic hardships and changes in the agriculture industry. Nearly hopeless, they set out for California's Central Valley along with thousands of other "Okies" in search of land, jobs and dignity.

Sutcliff, Rosemary. *The Outcast.* The story takes place in Roman Britain. An orphaned child, Beric, is shipwrecked off the coast of Dumnonia in Celtic Britain. He is rescued by a tribe that raises him. Beric struggles to belong as he contends with both acceptance and discrimination.

Taylor, Mildred D. *The Road to Memphis.* As America is on the brink of World War II, Cassie fights her own battle close to home. She dreams of college and law school. However, when her friend Moe lashes out at white tormentors, Cassie must help him leave their town in Mississippi.

Wallace Jason. *Out of Shadows.* Set in Zimbabwe in the 1980s, after the war for independence, a young English boy, Jacklin, is facing a dilemma. He witnessed compulsory land seizures by Robert Mugabe's government. Now, he is torn between his black friends at school and his sympathy for colonial whites. Robert plans a visit to the school and Jacklin learns that his white friend, Ivan, plans to assassinate the black leader. How does he solve this moral dilemma?

Catching Sight of the Past

The act of putting pen to paper encourages pause for thought,
this in turn makes us think more deeply about life,...
Norbet Platt

Genre: Fiction
Historical Fiction
Task Two: Writing a Character Sketch

A writer of historical fiction has to re-create the events and capture the essence of the characters in the narrative. The writer's essential tools to achieve these goals are imagination, diligence and solitude.

You have read an historical novel. Your task now is to write an academic essay, focusing on a critical analysis of an important character. Elaborate on your description with details and anchor general comments into specifics. Think about how the author began the novel. Who is telling the story? How is this important character introduced? Identify physical and personality traits.

Paragraph One
Introduction

Identify the title and author. Introduce the character by creating a "hook" to grab the reader's interest. This can be accomplished by making a general comment or including a quote from the novel. Two or three sentences will suffice.

Paragraph Two
Body Paragraph: Appearance and Personality Traits

For middle school students, describe the appearance of the main character, supported with details from the text. Do not simply list physical characteristics. **Discuss two** personality traits of the character. Refer to actions found in the text which show these traits.

For high school students, describe the appearance of the main character, supported with details from the novel. Do not simply list physical characteristics. **Discuss three** personality traits of the character and refer to actions found in the book which show these traits.

Paragraph Three
Body Paragraph: Initial Thoughts

What were your initial thoughts about the main character? Describe them. Focus on associations, speculations, feelings, concerns, issues and attitudes. Elaborate with details from the novel.

Paragraph Four
Body Paragraph: Afterthoughts

What were your afterthoughts? Were your initial thoughts and reactions altered by the end of the novel? Explain.

Paragraph Five
Closing Paragraph: Opinion

Write a closing paragraph discussing your opinion of the novel. For example, was the character's personality believable? What qualities of the author's writing style appealed to you? Support your ideas, whether positive or negative, from the text.

Assessment: Evaluation for this assignment will be based on thoughtful preparation and insightful comments.

Note to the Teacher

The following technique is offered to help middle school students remain on track for the completion of this assignment.

Middle School

Student Signature _____ Due Date_____

Parent Signature _____

Character Sketch Rubric Assessment

Content/Organization	Grade/Score

The student follows the directions for the assignment:
1. Title and Author in introduction
2. Reader's interest is effectively grabbed by "hook"
3. Character sketch included a description of physical characteristics and personality traits
4. Elaborate details used to present the character
5. Afterthought reflections explained
6. Essay ends with a sense of closure with opinion of the novel.

Mechanics	Grade/Score

The student edits the mechanics for the assignment:
1. Evidence of correct grammar and usage (example: agreement of subject and verb, correct sentence structure)
2. Correct punctuation
3. Correct spelling
4. Word choice: omitted "dead words" such as
   - verbs to be
   - get/got
5. Word choice: omitted "overused words" such as
   - awesome
   - amazing
   - awfully
   - great
   - a lot
   - stuff
   - very
   - nice

Note to the Teacher: This rubric is merely a suggestion. You may wish to modify it, to use one with which you are familiar or even to create one of your own.

Historical Fiction: Becoming the Character

The writer shakes up the familiar scene and,
as if by magic, we see a new meaning in it.
Anais Nin

Genre: Fiction
Historical Fiction
Task Three: Becoming the Character

You have studied the elements of historical fiction and have read a novel from this genre. The next step is to reflect and respond about this type of writing. Whether you have read *Mary, Bloody Mary; Summer of My German Soldier; Journey to America; A Break with Charity: A Story About the Salem Witch Trials; The Red Badge of Courage;* or *The Great Gatsby*, you will need to focus on several aspects of the novel:

- What in this historical novel is important?
- What did you find interesting about one of the main characters?
- What problems or conflicts did one of the characters face?
- How were these problems or conflicts resolved?

Your task is to select a character from the novel you have read and take on the **persona of the character** you selected. You become Mary Tudor, Anton, Lisa Platt, Sarah Bibber, Private Henry Fleming or Daisy. Be prepared to come to class dressed as your character. Give considerable thought and planning to your character's appearance and personality traits. Be creative, logical and reasonable! Before your presentation, provide the teacher with a detailed costume description and a list of any props to be used.

Oral Presentation: Guidelines
Time Limit: middle school -- two to three minutes.
high school -- three to five minutes.

Write out a final copy of the presentation of your persona and submit it to your teacher several days prior to your presentation. After reading it, your teacher may provide suggestions to improve your presentation. Once you have received feedback on your final copy, revise it, if necessary. Then memorize your persona for the presentation. Include the following guidelines in the content of your paper and in your oral presentation:

1. Introduction

    Introduce yourself and briefly discuss the historical period and the setting (time and place) of your novel.

2. Body

    Select no more than two problems or conflicts to present to the class. Discuss the events that led to these problems. Include detailed background information so the audience understands what happened. State the character's solution to each conflict in a confident manner. Provide logical reasons for the choices with examples of why the solutions did or did not work.

3. Conclusion

    Draw your presentation to a close. At the conclusion of your presentation, be prepared to respond to questions from the audience.

Written and Performance Assessment

Note: Distribute this assessment guide prior to the presentation.

Evaluation

Content of Written Presentation
1. The content follows the stated guidelines.
2. The introduction captures the audience's attention.
3. The body paragraphs are presented in a logical manner.
4. The content is supported with details.
5. The presentation ends with a sense of closure and is within the time limit.

Performance and Delivery
1. Knows the material thoroughly.
2. Uses appropriate expressions for the character.
3. Maintains eye contact.
4. Projects the voice, speak clearly and slowly.
5. Avoids **useless words** such as "um," "and," "like."
6. Appears at ease.

Note to the Teacher:
Consider allowing students to use notecards during the presentation. This option is left to the discretion of the teacher.

Historical Fiction: Becoming the Character

Notes to the Teacher:

   Consider the option of sharing in advance the method of assessment. Two grades may be given for assessment: one for content, one for delivery.

Assessment of Persona

Content: **Delivery:**

A+ The student **goes beyond** the instructions   Student knows the
     for the assignment and the presentation   material and presents
     is superbly organized. The costume is   it with confidence.
     appropriate and shows creativity.

A   Instructions are followed with supporting   Student knows the
     ideas. The presentation is outstanding   material and presents
     in regard to language and in organization.   it clearly.
     The costume is appropriate and creative.

B   Instructions are followed with a good   Student knows the
     introduction, body and conclusion.   material and presents
     Planning is evident for the costume.   it adequately.

C   Instructions are followed for the   Student appears less
     assignment but with fewer details.   familiar with content
     Costume fits the character.   and uses a few
                                                          "useless" words

D   Student attempts to follow instructions   Student does not know
     for the assignment. Little effort was   material and often
     made for the costume.   uses "useless" words.

Chapter 5

Gathering Thoughts

Gathering Thoughts
Reader's Response Log

But words are things, and a small drop of ink,
falling like dew upon a thought, produces
that which makes thousands, perhaps millions, think.
Lord Byron, 1788-1824

Genre: Fiction
The Novel

Notes to the Teacher

Effective teachers understand how important students' writing is to their academic growth. Students forming and expressing their own opinions about the literature they have read help them to become more perceptive readers and analytical thinkers. Students then feel that they have ownership of their ideas and their writing.

One of the methods available for students to have ownership of their ideas and their writing is the Reading Log. It is a challenging assignment that encourages student creativity.

Reading logs offer a unique way to help students integrate their personal reactions to what they read. They are commonly used in evaluating student insight. The premise involves the students' selecting a passage from the text, entering it in their log and responding to it. They wonder, they question, they make judgments or they may even reminisce about the passage.

Upon completion of the assignment, you may want to consider the following options:

- Cooperative Learning: Divide the class into groups.
- Ask each student to select one passage and response from his or her log to read to the group. Ask students in the group to comment regarding the student's selection and response.
- Ask for student volunteers to share one passage and their response with the class. Encourage feedback from the class.

Either option can pique the interest of other students to read the novel presented.

Reading List

A reading list is not provided for this assignment, as in other assignments. For this assignment, whether elementary school, middle school or high school, encourage students to select a novel of their own choosing in an area of their own interest. In addition, they need to select a novel appropriate to their grade level.

Assessment

Assessment is left to the discretion of the teacher. However, we suggest using one of the following:

- A letter grade for content and one for mechanics along with a brief written commentary by the teacher.
- A rubric of your choosing, one specifically developed for this assignment or a generic rubric.

Gathering Thoughts
Reader's Response Log

...the profit of books is according to the sensibility of the reader; the profoundest thought or passion sleeps as in a mine, until it is discovered by an equal mind and heart.
Ralph Waldo Emerson

Genre: Fiction
The Novel
Task One: Reading the Novel

You have selected and have read a novel of your choice and are ready to complete Task Two, a Reader's Response Log.

Task Two: Gathering Thoughts
A Writer's Desk

Introduction

A Reader's Response Log is designed to help you become more aware of your own thought processes and to respond to what you have read. Logs are concise, factual in content and personal in tone. This is an opportunity for you to express freely your own thoughts and ideas. The process for this assignment involves **selecting three passages from your novel, recording them accurately in your log and responding to them.**

You may question, make predictions, form judgments or reminisce about how this passage relates to you personally. In addition, you may comment on or react to the title, to the illustrations, to the word choice or to phrases or topic sentences you find significant.

Procedure

Be sure to record each passage accurately and include the page number for each passage. The heading of the Reader's Log must include the following for the novel:

Title
Author
Publishing Company
Number of Pages

Select one of the following options:
Option A

1. **Divide your paper** into two columns.
2. On the left side, indicate the **page number** followed by **an accurate recording** of the passage.
3. On the right side, write the word **"Response"** and below it, write your reactions to the passage.

Option B

1. Indicate the **page number**, followed by an **accurate recording** of the passage.
2. Under the passage, write **"Response"** and below it **write your reactions**. **Suggestion:** use black ink for your passage and another color (except yellow) for your response. Whichever you choose, be consistent in the format.

Your responses may begin by using any of the following "sentence openers" or ones of your own creation:

I believe…
I realize…
I agree/disagree…
I think…
I expected…
I am shocked…
I am bewildered…
In reflection…
It disturbs me…
How could that …
Why did…
That's impossible!
Who would have thought…
How ironic…
When that happens…
It is a curious fact…
So this is it?
The author's choice of words made me…

A few of the "sentence openers" lead the reader to a critical analysis. If so, write down your ideas or impressions to any aspect of the novel: plot, characters, theme or even the author's style. Other "sentence openers" necessitate an emotional response or connection to your life. If this is the case, write your own ideas and impressions regarding the passage. Keep in mind that the goal of a Reader's Log is to help you deepen your understanding of the text and to connect what you read to your own life. As Samuel Taylor Coleridge remarked, "Force yourself to reflect on what you read, paragraph by paragraph."

Chapter 6

It's True. . .this time it's personal

It's True…
this time it's personal

One writes to make a home for one's self,
on paper, in time, in others' minds.
Alfred Kazin
Writer and Literary Critic

Genre: Non-Fiction
Introduction

Non-fiction is prose writing about ideas, real people, places or events. In reading non-fiction, the reader may read books that provide challenging ideas, suspense and even humor. As you read, reflect on the author's purpose: Is it to entertain? It is to inform? Is it to persuade you to see things from a different perspective? Or is it to find out about the world and more about yourself?

Literary non-fiction includes the following categories:

Autobiography: An autobiography is the story of one's life as told by the writer. It is written from the first person point of view.

Example: *Up from Slavery* by Booker T. Washington.

Biography: A biography is the story of a person's life written by someone else. The writer must do research from letters, diaries, books and any other information pertinent to the person's life and, when possible, interview the subject.

Example: *Son of the Morning Star: Custer and the Little Big Horn* by Evan Connell.

Diary: A diary tells what occurs during a specific time frame and includes a record of specific incidents and observations. It may be kept daily or written at frequent intervals.

Examples: *Linotte: The Early Diary of Anais Nin 1914-1920* by Anais Nin.

Diary of Ann Frank by Ann Frank.

Journal: A journal tells the reader that the author recorded incidents as they occurred and may include the thoughts and feeling of the author as well as objective details.

Example: *Walden Pond* by Henry David Thoreau.

Memoir: A memoir allows the author to select events and images that reveal significant things about himself/herself. The challenge in writing a memoir is to find out how specific moments connect, forming a pattern in the author's life. The author of a memoir must present the selected images in a vivid and convincing manner, as if they happened yesterday. The author, Eleanor Ramrath Garner, comments, "Memoirs are in essence historical documents. They are timeless perennials that not only describe a period of history, but also address the universality of collective human experiences."

Examples: *Eleanor's Story: An American Girl in Hitler's Germany*
by Eleanor Ramrath Garner.
MEMOIR The Stutterer Speaks by Gene Pepper

It's True...
this time it's personal

Life is a story filled with meanderings, sudden twists and turns. Yet, hidden in the details of everyday living are autobiographical and memoir subjects of universal appeal and interest.

Genre: Non-Fiction
Task One: Selecting and Reading Non-fiction

You have reviewed the different types of literary non-fiction. However, for this assignment, the focus is on autobiography and memoir. From the list below or a selection of your own, read an autobiography or a memoir. Following the reading of the book, you will complete the task that connects with the type of book you read.

AUTOBIOGRAPHY

Ali, Muhammad. *The Soul of the Butterfly.* *The Soul of a Butterfly* is a "spiritual biography," in which Muhammad Ali tells the philosophy by which he lives his life. With the assistance of his daughter Hana, Ali writes about those things that have inspired and modeled him. He writes about love, ambitions, God, life and the responsibilities of power and fame.

Amothy, Christine. *I Am Fifteen—and I Don't Want to Die.* Christine Amothy is fifteen when she is caught in the middle of a war in Budapest, Hungary. While hiding in the cellar of their bombed out apartment building, Christine and her family fear for their lives. Through this experience, Christine learns some difficult lessons about life, death and the struggles to survive the horrors of war.

Angelou, Maya. *I Know Why the Caged Bird Sings.* Maya Angelou richly pens an autobiography of her childhood in Arkansas. She writes about her childhood in the south in the 1930's and 1940's. She learns the power of the whites and experiences a terrible trauma. As a black woman, she was known not only discrimination and abject poverty but also hope, joy, celebration and achievement.

Burnett, Carol. *Carol Burnett.* This autobiography about and by television and Broadway star Carol Burnett tells of her childhood, living in Hollywood with her grandmother during the Depression. She tells of her sometimes hilarious, sometimes not so hilarious experiences growing up and the emergence of her comedic talents, among others.

Cronkite, Walter. *A Reporter's Life.* Newscaster Walter Cronkite's autobiography tells about the dozens of "scoops" he covered during his television news broadcasting years. He witnessed and participated in many of the 20th century's most memorable major events. In addition, Cronkite describes the transformation of network television as a vehicle that has become a major force in forming American consciousness.

Hamilton, Bethany. *Soul Surfer: A True Story of Faith, Family, and Fighting to Get Back on the Board.* Bethany Hamilton is a teenage surfer who lost her arm in a shark attack off the coast of Kauai, Hawaii, and returns to surfing, the sport she loves. The loss of her arm in a horrific shark attack could not come between her and the waves.

Hakakian, Roya. *Journey from the Land of No: A Girlhood Caught in Revolutionary Iran.* Roya Hakakian recalls with candor and verve her childhood and adolescence in pre-revolutionary Iran. With an open heart and often with great humor, she re-creates a time and place dominated by religious fanaticism, violence and fear

Hamm, Mia. *Go for the Goal: A Champion's Guide to Winning in Soccer and Life.* *Go for the Goal* is not only the inspiring story of how Mia became a global terror with a soccer ball but also a guide for any youth with the all-American dream of making the team and becoming a champion.

Keller, Helen. *The Story of My Life.* *The Story of My Life* is the first book Helen Keller wrote. The autobiography reflects Helen's life from an early age until her graduation from Radcliffe College and explains how she overcame her visual and hearing disabilities.

Kennedy, Michelle. *Without a Net: Middle Class and Homeless (with Kids) in America.* Growing up in a middle-class family in Vermont, Michelle Kennedy leaves home to begin college at American University in Washington, D.C., and interns as a U.S. Senate page. She has a boyfriend, Tom, whom she adores and soon marries; they move into a starter apartment in the suburbs. But, the life Michelle was building suddenly unravels, and by age 24, she finds herself single, homeless, and living out of a car with her three small children. Michelle Kennedy's autobiography tells what happens when the American Dream comes apart.

Meyers, Walter Dean. *Bad Boy.* From bad boy to role model, Meyers recalls growing up in Harlem in the 1940's and 1950's, when seeing Langston Hughes and Sugar Ray Robinson on the street was the norm and Jackie Robinson ruled the baseball field.

O'Connor, Sandra Day. *Sandra Day O'Connor.* This is the story of Sandra Day O'Connor's life, including her learning about work and people and her rise to the position of the first female justice on the U. S. Supreme Court. Laced throughout are stories about three generations of the Day family.

Ohno, Apolo Anton. *A Journey: the Autobiography of Apolo Anton Ohno.* In an autobiography, this controversial young American writes about his career, including his winning gold and silver medals in speed skating at the 2002 Winter Olympics.

Paul, Caroline. *Fighting Fire: A Personal Story.* She fought the prejudice. She fought the stereotype. Then she fought the greatest force of all -- fire. When the San Francisco Fire Department broke the rule never to hire women, Caroline Paul never thought she would be the chosen one.

Pfetzer, Mark. *Within Reach: My Everest Story.* The author describes how he spent his teenage years climbing mountains in the United States, South America, Africa and Asia, with an emphasis on his two expeditions up Mount Everest.

Spinelli, Jerry. *Knots in My Yo-Yo String.* This Italian-American Newbery Medalist presents a humorous account of his childhood and youth in Norristown, Pennsylvania, as he learns the spectacular spinning moves of the yo-yo.

Tada, Joni Earechson. *Joni: An Unforgettable Story.* This is an award-winning story of a young woman diver who triumphed over devastating odds to touch countless lives the world over with a healing message.

ten Boom, Corrie. *The Hiding Place.* Corrie ten Boom tells about her life in Holland and how she became the heroine of the Resistance. During World War II, she and her family risked their lives to help Jews escape from the Nazis but were captured and sent to the infamous Nazi death camps. Only Carrie survived to tell the story of how faith ultimately triumphs over evil.

Washington, Booker T. *Up from Slavery.* *Up from Slavery* chronicles over 50 years of Washington's life: from slave to schoolmaster to the face of southern race relations. Throughout, he stresses the importance of education for the Black population as a reasonable tactic to ease race relations in the South.

Welty, Eudora. *One Writer's Beginnings.* Eudora Welty, an extraordinary woman and author, writes in her autobiography about the things that influenced her writing. She relates stories of her childhood, her parents' childhood experiences, her early years as an adult and her parents' emphasis on family history, learning and reading.

Wozniak, Steve. *iWoz: Computer Geek to Cult Icon: How I Invented the Personal Computer, Co-Founded Apple, and Had Fun Doing It.* Steve Wozniak tells his story of revolutionizing the computer world with his invention of the personal computer. As the sole inventor of the Apple I and II computers, Wozniak has enjoyed wealth, fame and the most coveted awards an engineer can receive.

MEMOIR

Baker, Russell. *Growing Up.* Russell Baker's sad, but amusing memoir recounts his growing up in rural Virginia during the Great Depression and his young adult life with his mother, living in Baltimore.

Bryson, Bill. *A Walk in the Woods. Rediscovering America on the Appalachian Trail.* As Bryson and his friend Katz walk the 2,100 miles from Georgia to Maine, the reader is treated to both a very funny personal memoir and a delightful chronicle of the trail, the people who created it, and the places it passes through.

Buchwald, Art. *I'll Always Have Paris.* American humorist Art Buchwald dazzles the readers with his memories, living in Paris in the late 1940's and 1950's. Clashing with police in Paris, running the bulls in Pamplona, Spain, and dining with gangsters in Naples, Art Buchwald reports on the foibles of the elite members of the international society.

Champlin, Charles. *Back There Where the Past Was: A Small-Town Boyhood.* In his memoir, well-known film critic Charles Champlin recounts his first 16 years growing up in Hammonsport, New York, during the Great Depression. This memoir is full of humorous and revealing confessions.

Dahl, Roald. *Boy: Tales of Childhood.* Roald Dahl presents humorous anecdotes from his childhood, which includes summer vacations in Norway and his years in an English boarding school.

Dinesen, Isak. *Out of Africa.* This memoir recounts events of the seventeen years when Blixen made her home in Kenya, then British East Africa. It is a vivid snapshot of African colonial life in the last decades of the British Empire.

Doran, Phil. *The Reluctant Tuscan: How I Discovered My Inner Italian.* Phil Doran writes an informative, comic and poignant memoir about his midlife adventures and his move to Italy. His witty tone and amusing accounts . . . keep the readers "hooked" as they learn how he rediscovers himself and his marriage and gets in touch with his inner Italian.

Gardner, Eleanor Ramrath. *Eleanor's Story: An American Girl in Hitler's Germany.* A gifted story teller, Eleanor Gardner tells her story of struggles to survive as an American girl in Nazi Germany. Her family faces threats from the Gestapo, separation and the final battle for Berlin.

Grant, Ulysses S. *Personal Memoirs of Ulysses S. Grant.* Grant wrote an impressive memoir about his boyhood in Ohio, his graduation from West Point and his actions during the American Civil War. Written under difficult circumstances, as he was dying of terminal cancer, he completed the task in 1885 and died several days later. His publisher, Mark Twain, published the two-volume set shortly after Grant's death.

Horett. Norene. *Main Street Was Two Blocks Long.* Norene Horett writes about growing up in Carnegie, Oklahoma, in the 1940's and 1950's. She introduces unforgettable people and places that shaped her memories. She describes the joys and sorrows of the people of this small town.

Katz, Jon. *A Dog Year: Twelve Months, Four Dogs and Me.* This is a warm, humorous and moving memoir of the enriching and ennobling experience of living with Labradors and a Border Collie.

Kimmel, Haven. *A Girl Named Zippy: Growing Up Small in Mooreland, Indiana.* In this lovingly-told memoir, Kimmel takes readers back in time to when small-town America was still trapped in the amber of the innocent post-war period—people helped their neighbors, went to church, and kept barnyard animals in their backyards.

Kramer, Clara. *Clara's War: One Girl's Story of Survival.* This heart-stopping story of a young girl hiding from the Nazis is based on Clara Kramer's diary of her years surviving in an underground bunker with 17 other people.

Martinez, Al. *I'll Be Damned If I'll Die in Oakland: A Sort of Travel Memoir.* In *I'll Be Damned if I'll Die in Oakland*, popular *Los Angeles Times* columnist Al Martinez takes the reader on a funny, crazy, surprising and sometimes poignant three-month ride around the globe with his wife, his children, his grandchildren and his dog.

McCourt, Frank. *Angela's Ashes.* This 1996 Pulitzer Prize winning book is a chronicle of Frank McCourt's childhood in Ireland. With brilliant writing and touches of humor, the memoir allows the reader to see the author's triumphs also.

Morris, Willie. *Good Old Boy.* This book chronicles the wonder and excitement of growing up in the small town of Yazoo, Mississippi. Willie Morris writes about his family and friends, Bubba and Billy, and the pranks they played and about his dog, named Old Skip, as well.

Nor, Ehud. *Lost Childhood: A World War II Memoir.* This memoir describes six years in the life of a daring and resourceful Polish Jewish boy and his family, who survived the Holocaust by using false papers and posing as Catholics.

Pepper, Gene. *Memoir: The Stutterer Speaks.* The heartwarming memoir tells of Gene Pepper's youth growing up in Salt Lake City. He recounts his challenges and painful experiences at school, tormented by bullies. Overcoming his obstacles, including stuttering and low self-esteem, his reminisces include traditional family celebrations, his university days at Stanford and his experiences as a U. S. Marine.

Salzman, Mark. *True Notebooks: A Writer's Year at Juvenile Hall.* Teaching writing to seventeen-year-olds detained in Los Angeles Central Juvenile Hall, Salzman finds himself surprised by the boys' talent. The teens' heartwarming, funny voices are included in this irresistible, provocative memoir.

Thurber, James. *My Life and Hard Times.* James Thurber reflects on his own life growing up in Columbus, Ohio. With humor and razor wit, Thurber writes about the chaos and frustrations of his family, boyhood, youth, dogs and the imperfections of human nature.

Toth, Susan Allen. *How to Prepare for Your High-School Reunion and Other Midlife Musings.* In this memoir about growing up in a small town, Susan Toth writes about her life and the struggles and joys she encounters. The essays cover many topics and familiar themes emerge, reflecting on her life as a single woman, wife, mother, teacher and writer.

Unger, Zac. *Working Fire: the Making of an Accidental Fireman.* This funny and moving memoir is about one man's coming into his calling and his transformation from ambivalent Ivy League grad to skilled and dedicated firefighter.

Wooden, John and Steve Jamison. *Wooden: A Lifetime of Observations and Reflections On and Off the Court.* "I am just a common man who is true to his beliefs," says John Wooden of himself. With the help of Steve Jameson, a noted author and authority on the life and leadership of John Wooden, Wooden offers his wisdom as a highly respected and admired basketball coach and his personal philosophy regarding family, achievement and success.

It's True...
this time it's personal

Today you are you! That is truer than true!
There is no one alive who is you-er than you!
Dr. Seuss

Genre: Non-Fiction
Task Two: **Writing an Autobiographical Incident**
My Life Re-visited

Having read an autobiography, which is the story of one's life as told by the writer, your task now is to reflect on your own life's story and re-visit it.

Writing about our life experiences and sharing those experiences enables us to better understand our past. The reminiscences about an incident allows us to delight in discovery and opens our minds to creativity and even change.

Think about your life and reflect upon a specific incident. It could be funny, exciting, insightful, sad, scary, unexpected or just interesting to you.

Autobiographical incidents focus more on content and insight and less on style.

Getting Started

The following guidelines are **suggested** for writing an autobiographical incident.

Brainstorm Ideas

- Reflect on ideas, associations of words or images connected with an incident.
- Select an event and focus on your subject and write for several minutes without making judgments.

Developing the Draft

You are encouraged to be original, creative and even playful with your ideas. Feel free to exaggerate or use hyperbole. Help the reader *see* the incident. What happened? Who was involved? Where did the incident take place? Why did you act that way?

Here are a few writing strategies:

Introduction: Paragraph One

Introduce the topic and make the reader interested in what you have to say by creating a hook.

- Begin with a question.
- Begin with a sentence having two or three descriptive words or phrases.
- Use a quote.

Body Paragraph: Paragraph Two

Describe the main event of the incident. Include specific details to help the reader visualize actions and setting. **Do not just "tell" a feeling**.

Add dialogue to enhance the narrative.

Body Paragraph: Paragraph Three

What was the outcome of this incident? Describe it in detail.

Conclusion: Paragraph Four

What did you learn from this experience? Include your reflections.

Leave the reader with a final thought (a zinger!).

Revising the Draft

Read the draft to add or subtract details, to substitute words or to rearrange the order of the content. Through this process, remember the goal is to "pull" the reader into your story.

Editing/Proofreading the Draft

Edit the final copy of your autobiographical incident. Focus on the "surface correctness" of the writing: grammar, punctuation and spelling.

Proofread your writing carefully to check for additional errors and to make the necessary corrections

Title Your Autobiographical Incident

Titles are very important. Write the title for this assignment after the final draft has been completed. Let your title emanate from the content.

It's True...
this time it's personal
Autobiographical Incident
My Life Re-visited

Notes to the Teacher

You may want the students to share the final draft of their autobiographical incident. Their autobiographical incident may be read to a partner or in a group of no more than four. In addition, a group member may suggest that a student share his or her piece of writing with the entire class.

This assignment will require thoughtful preparation for students. It is reasonable to assume that students will expect or want an assessment of their final copy. The method for assessment is the teacher's choice. We, however, suggest a letter grade for content and another grade for mechanics, along with written comments.

It's True...
this time it's personal

The events in our lives happen in a sequence in time,
but in their significance to ourselves, they find their
own order... the continuous thread of revelation.
                                                    Eudora Welty

Genre: Non-Fiction
Task Two: Writing a Memoir
Collecting Memories

Though our lives may feel mundane and sometimes even monotonous and seemingly insignificant, beneath each experience is material that offers universal appeal. So begins your memoir – a reflection on those significant follies, hilarities, poignancies, wonders, ironies, joys and losses. And, it's all true!

A memoir focuses more on content and insight and less on structure.

Getting Started

Having read a memoir, which consists of selected events and images that recall significant milestones in the author's life, you are now asked to write your own memoir.

In your memoir include any three of the reflections listed above in the **first paragraph.** Focus on specific memories or events. Recall vivid incidents that were emotional. Then "see" the experience again and try to relive it. As author Gene Pepper suggests, "Think small and begin from there, wherever 'there' is for you."

Possible Topics as a Springboard for Writing your Memoir

- Saved money to buy…
- First day at school
- Favorite pet
- A punishment you did or did not deserve
- A sport
- A memorable trip
- The "best" or "worst" teacher
- My "best" or "worst" friend
- My favorite toy
- I was scared of …
- When I played make-believe, I pretended…
- When I was a child, the person I felt close to…
- My first date
- My first kiss
- My first car
- A Right of Passage
- I daydreamed about…
- A good or bad report card

- A spanking
- A trip to the dentist
- A birthday party
- A game we used to play
- A responsibility I had
- My summer job
- The day I showed my independence

Developing the Draft

The following guidelines are **suggestions** for writing a memoir:

1. Brainstorm Ideas
   - Create a cluster of ideas, associations of words or images.

     or

   - Use a reporter's style, listing the 5 W's +How questions to start your ideas flowing.
2. Narrow the topics to three selections from the cluster or list.
3. Focus on each topic and select the most significant details and write for several minutes without making judgments. Don't spend time "thinking".
   Begin writing when an idea triggers your imagination. Be spontaneous!
4. Add dialogue to enhance your narrative.
5. Review the **three entries** and determine if there is theme or pattern emerging in the account of your memories? Do you see an importance in that pattern? Do you see your "history" coming alive? Does it provide "the texture, the details, the sights, the sounds, the smells and, above all, the emotions of important events in the past?" (Eleanor Ramrath Garner).

Revising the Draft

Read the draft to add or subtract details, to substitute words or to rearrange the order of the content. Through this process, remember the goal is to "pull" the reader into your story.

Editing/Proofreading the Draft

You are now ready to edit and then proofread the final copy of your memoir. Focus on the "surface correctness" of the writing: grammar, punctuation and spelling.

Re-read your writing carefully to check for additional errors and to make the necessary corrections.

Title Your Memoir

Titles are very important. Write the title for your memoir after the final draft has been completed. Let the title emanate from the content. Be original and creative!

It's True...
this time it's personal
Writing a Memoir
Collecting Memories

Notes to the Teacher

You may want the students to share the final draft of their memoir. Their memoirs may be read to a partner or in a group of no more than four. In addition, a group member may suggest that a student share his or her piece of writing with the entire class.

This assignment will require thoughtful preparation for students. It is reasonable to assume that students will expect or want an assessment of their final copy. The method for assessment is the teacher's choice. We, however, suggest a letter grade for content and another grade for mechanics, along with written comments.

It's True...
this time it's personal
Coat of Arms

Genre: Non-fiction
Task Three: Designing Your Own Coat of Arms

A coat of arms is a heraldic design on a shield or surcoat. The design represents a symbol of an individual person. It has been used to cover, protect and identify the person wearing it. Coats of arms are still used today by institutions, by families and by individuals.

As a final task, you are asked to design a **coat of arms crest** unique to yourself. A coat of arms (crest) is included in this section to enable you to complete this assignment. Note that the outline is divided into four sections, plus a space below the drawing for your motto.

Plan your coat of arms keeping in mind these topics:
1. A talent
2. A hobby or interest
3. A sport or musical instrument
4. A metaphor: Select an animal, a tree, a lake or any other object that identifies you.
5. Your motto: Create your own motto.

Here are some ideas for a motto:
- Patience yields the light of understanding. (William Shakespeare...*ROMEO AND JULIET)*
- Spread your hopes. (William Shakespeare...*THE MERCHANT OF VENICE*)
- Talents are best nurtured in solitude. (Goethe)
- Goodness is the only investment that never fails. (Henry David Thoreau)
- Do all the good you can. (John Wesley)
- Exuberance is beauty. (William Blake)
- Deep in their roots, all flowers keep the light. (Theodore Roethke)

Suggestions for completing the assignment:
1. Except for the placement of the motto, the artwork can be done in any order.
2. Use 80% to 90% of the space.
3. Select no more than **three or four** colors for the design.
4. Use black fine line felt pens or colored pencils for the designing of the motto. Write the motto at the bottom of the crest in the scroll.

Notes to the Teacher:
Invite students to share their coat of arms with the class. Display their coat of arms in the classroom.

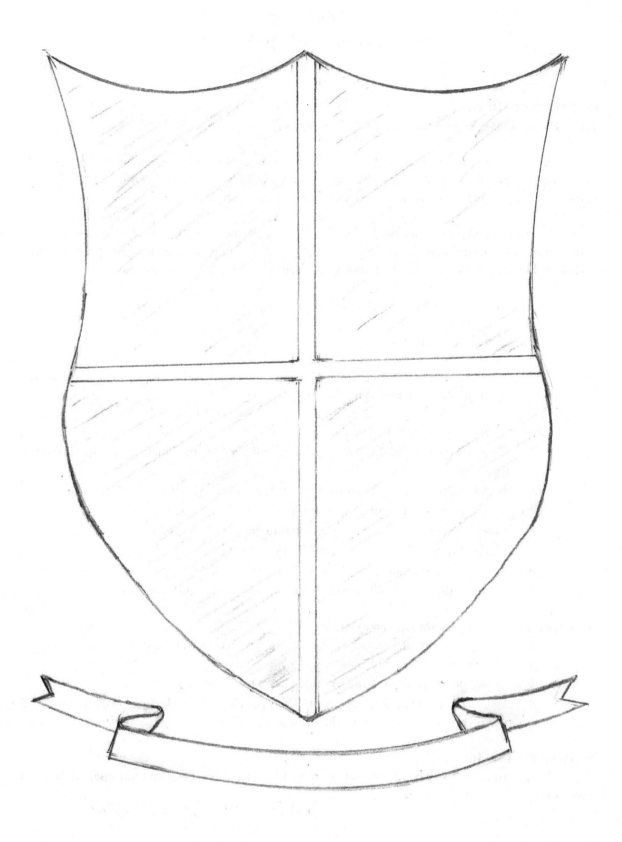

Chapter 7

Another Writer's Beginnings

Another Writer's Beginnings

The books that help you the most are those which
make you think the most...

Theodore Parker
Scholar, Clergyman, Abolitionist

Genre: Non-fiction
Extraordinary Lives
The Art and Craft of Biography

Introduction

Among the selections of literary non-fiction is the genre of biography. It is the story of someone's life told by another. The writer of biography has the responsibility to conduct extensive research on the person's life: reading books, reading diaries, reading letters and even interviewing the subject, if possible.

The goal of the biographer is to reveal for the reader the "whole human being," experiencing sudden joys and the bitter darkness of life. The writer probes deeply into the subject's psyche, presenting an intimate portrait. The biographer seeks to present an honest portrait of the subject. Yet, being totally objective is an unrealistic and even impossible goal.

A biography may be read on several levels, such as an enthralling story with the elements of a sweeping novel, a social history or a life intensively lived. Reading a biography can be fun!

Another Writer's Beginnings...

Genre: Non-Fiction
Extraordinary Lives
The Art and Craft of Biography
Task One of Three: Reading and Note taking

Select and read a biography of your choice from the list provided or one of your own. While reading the biography, your assignment is to abstract ideas from the book. Copy words, phrases and sentences from the text that strike you as important elements of the narrative. Keep these notes since you will attach them to the final task.

Your teacher will determine how much time you have to select your book, to read it and to write the notes.

Biography

Albom, Mitch. *Tuesdays with Morrie: an Old Man, a Young Man, and Life's Greatest Lesson.* Was it a grandparent, a teacher, a colleague or someone older, patient and wise who understood you when you were young? Wouldn't you like to see that person again, ask the bigger questions that still haunt you? For Mitch Albom, that person was Morrie Schwartz, his beloved college professor. Mitch Albom has a second chance to ask the big questions of life.

Allen, Paula Gunn. *Pocahontas.* In striking counterpoint to the conventional account, *Pocahontas* is a bold biography that tells the story of the beloved Indian maiden from a Native American perspective. Dr. Paula Gunn Allen, the acknowledged founder of Native American literary studies, draws on sources and remarkable new insights into the adventurous life and role of this American heroine.

Barrett, Mary Ellen. *Irving Berlin.* This reminiscent biography by Irving Berlin's daughter tells of the life of a Russian-born Jewish cantor and his private life, his contented childhood, his friends, his successes in NYC, California and the Catskills.

Berg, A. Scott. *Lindberg.* This highly distinguished biography tells of the life of Charles Lindberg, his one-man transatlantic flight in 1927, and the kidnapping and death of his son in 1932. These events have resulted in a continuing fascination with the man and his life today.

Berg, A. Scott. *Max Perkins: Editor of Genius.* Recipient of the National Book Review Award, Scott Berg explores the professional and personal life of editor Maxwell Perkins, who guided many writers, including F. Scott Fitzgerald, Ernest Hemingway, Thomas Wolfe and James Jones, among others.

Berg, A. Scott. *Samuel Goldwyn.* This biography portrays the life of one of Hollywood's legendary magnates who held a special place in the film industry. Berg writes about Goldwyn's first business venture in 1913 and the events that led to his breaking away and forming his own production company.

Brookhiser, Richard. *George Washington on Leadership.* Richard Brookhiser's biography examines the details of George Washington's life and explains his management and leadership style, called the "hub-and-spoke system." Washington made mistakes in his career; however, he learned from them. He was a superb communicator and learned how to master his temper and how to handle people.

Carpenter, Humphrey; edited by J. R. R. Tolkien. *J.R.R. Tolkien: A Biography.* This is a biography of the creator of Middle-earth. One day Tolkien's life changed. While grading essay papers, he found himself writing, "In a hole in the ground there lived a hobbit" -- and worldwide renown awaited him.

Chapman, Matthew. *Trials of the Monkey.* This stimulating biography, by Darwin's great-great-grandson, tells of Chapman's travels to Dayton, Tennessee. He wants to see if opinions have changed since the 'monkey trial" about the teaching of evolution in the schools. There, he is confronted not only by fundamentalist beliefs that banish the theory of evolution but also by his own atheism.

Cox. Clinton. *Houdini: Master of Illusion.* This biography of famed magician and illusionist Harry Houdini explores how he carried out his amazing feats and exposes the secrets behind many of his tricks. The author cites Houdini's brilliance, physical dexterity and wild imagination as factors that made him a true master of illusion.

Connell, Evan. *Son of the Morning Star: Custer and the Little Big Horn.* *Son of the Morning Star* is a book about General George Armstrong Custer. The book chronicles the Battle of Little Bighorn, the personalities involved and the events leading up to and following it.

Dash, Joan and Dusan Petricic. *A Dangerous Engine: Benjamin Franklin, from Scientist to Diplomat.* This biography about Benjamin Franklin focuses on his first-love – science — as well as on his 25 years as an American statesman. His experiments with electricity made him famous in Europe long before they were successful. Franklin became America's first foreign diplomat, later helping to secure France's military and financial support for the American Revolution.

Davenport, Marsha. *Mozart.* With letters, original documents and others telling their own stories, Marsha Davenport presents a realistic and outstanding portrait of the 18th century composer, Mozart. Her biography presents him as a man of commanding stature.

Davis, Sampson. *The Pact: Three Young Men Make a Promise and Fulfill a Dream.* Because of their determination, three black teenagers from a rough part of Newark, New Jersey, vow to finish college together. In order to refrain from returning to the streets, they make a pact to rely on each other. They survive college and complete medical school.

Edwards, Anne. *Maria Callas.* One of the greatest, if not the greatest, opera singers of the last century was Maria Callas. Her biography is a story about her extraordinary life and the mystery of her death. Anne Edwards tells about Maria Callas and her loves, her life and her passion for opera.

Emerson, Jason. *Madness of Mary Lincoln.* Jason Emerson's biography of Mary Todd Lincoln, wife of President Abraham Lincoln, is an historical masterpiece and enthralling story about her mental illness and President Lincoln's understanding of it and the degree to which he aided her in maintaining stability. In addition, the biography follows her life after the President's assassination: her severe depression and physical ailments and the effect of her son's death on her.

Flynn, Raymond. *John Paul II.* Raymond Flynn, former U. S. ambassador to the Vatican, provides an inspiring and intimate view of Pope John Paul II. With the author's understanding of the inner workings of Catholicism, the role of politics and his personal contacts with the Pope, Flynn relates how John Paul II changed the papacy.

Fradin, Dennis and Judith Fradin. *Fight On!: Mary Church Terrell's Battle for Integration.* This biography recounts the tale of a girl born to slaves in 1865, a girl who went on to become an early civil rights leader with a career spanning 60 years. She was the first black woman to serve on the Washington, D.C., Board of Education and a cofounder of the NAACP.

Fraser, Antonia. *Marie Antoinette.* This brilliantly written biography gives the reader a gripping and intense account of the 18th century French queen whose lavish living and desires became legendary. Antonia Frazer presents Marie Antoinette as a figure whose road to the guillotine was partly the result of her innocence as well as the political and social system of pre-Revolutionary France.

Freedman, Russell. *Eleanor Roosevelt: A Life of Discovery.* This story of Eleanor Roosevelt traces the life of the former First Lady from her early childhood through the tumultuous years in the White House to her active role in the founding of the United Nations after World War II.

Green, Julien. *God's Fool: The Life of Francis of Assisi.* Attempting to portray the complex personality of Saint Francis, Julien Green looks at his early life. He researches his influences and discusses the rules he developed for the Franciscan order of monks.

Greene, Bob. *Duty.* This is the biography of three lives connected by history, proximity and blood. It is the story of Paul Tibbets, who Bob Greene's father says had "won the war." Green traces the steps that Tibbets undertook at the age of 29 to assemble a team of 1800 American soldiers to carry out what has become known as the most violent act of man.

Gunther, Vanessa. *Chief Joseph: A Biography.* *Chief Joseph: A Biography* explores the world of the Nez Perce Indians from their entrance into the Columbia Plateau through their relations with the expanding United States. It shows how Chief Joseph shepherded his people through the ordeals that confronted them, including the loss of their land, the loss of their freedom and the persistent threats to them.

Hertog, Susan. *Anne Morrow Lindbergh.* Loyal wife, devoted mother, pioneering aviator and highly respected author, Anne Morrow Lindbergh's life is revealed through interviews, diaries, letters and other documents. Susan Hertog presents a biography of a woman whose triumphs, struggles and perseverance captured the attention of the public.

Hillenbrand, Laura. *Unbroken; A World War II Story of Survival, Resilience, and Redemption.* This is the biography of World War II American bombardier Louis Zamperini's 47-day experiences of survival, of starvation and later his capture as a POW by the Japanese. Laura Hillenbrand also writes of his participation in the Berlin Olympics in 1936 and almost setting a record for the four-minute mile.

Hirsch, James. S. Hurricane: *The Miraculous Journey of Rubin Carter.* This is a biography of a black boxer named Rubin "Hurricane" Carter and his young acquaintance John Artis. They were convicted of three murders by an all-white jury in 1947. Claiming he was innocent, Carter was able to prove his innocence and was freed in 1976 pending a new trial. He lost his appeal and was returned to prison. With the help of a teenager and a group of Canadians, he still wages a battle to prove his innocence and to gain his freedom.

Hirschson, Stanley P. *General Patton.* In this biography of General George Patton, Stanley P. Hirschson presents a portrait of Patton as a complex soldier, not only a brilliant military strategist but also a bold communicator. While researching Patton's life, Hirschson discovered documents about civilian and military massacres in Sicily and his relationships with top Allied generals.

Hohler, Robert T. *I Touch the Future.* Robert Hohler writes an account of the life, teaching career, NASA training and impact of Christa McAuliffe, the woman who was selected to be the first teacher in space.

Hoose, Phillip. *Claudette Colvin: Twice Toward Justice.* This biography is about an unknown civil rights teenager named Claudette Colvin. She became a civil rights leader when she refused to give up her seat on a bus to a white woman in Alabama in 1955. Unlike Rosa Parks, Claudette Colvin found herself ignored and rejected by community leaders. She becomes the key plaintiff in *Browder v. Gayle*, the landmark case that struck down the segregation laws of Montgomery, thus changing the course of American history.

Kimmel, Elizabeth Cody. *Boy on a Throne.* This biography focuses on the childhood of the Dalai Lama, who rose from humble beginnings to become a world leader. This dramatic biographic narrative traces his childhood and, in doing so, tells the story of Tibet.

Lee, Carol Ann. *Friend Called Anne: One Girl's Story of War, Peace, and a Unique Friendship with Anne Frank.* This is a story of Jacqueline van Maarsen ("Jopie"), who was Anne Frank's best friend before Anne went into hiding. She remembers her friendship with Anne, her own experiences of the Holocaust and her acceptance of the fame of Anne's diary.

McMurtry, Larry. *Crazy Horse: A Life.* This biography looks back more than 120 years at the life and death of the Sioux warrior who became a leader at the Battle of Little Bighorn in Montana. A mythic figure, Crazy Horse emerges from McMurtry's sensitive portrait as the poignant hero of an epoch.

Meachum, Virginia. *Steven Spielberg: Hollywood Filmmaker.* This biography explores the life and career of the successful filmmaker. It begins with his childhood and includes discussions of his projects as a director, writer and producer.

Morgan, Judith and Neil. *Dr. Seuss & Mr. Geisel: A Biography.* Horton, Thidwick, Yertle, the Lorax, the Grinch, Sneetches and the Cat in the Hat are just a handful of the bizarre and beloved characters Theodor S. Geisel (1904–1991), alias Dr. Seuss, created in his 47 books written for children.

Morris, Edmund. *The Rise of Theodore Roosevelt.* Described by the *Chicago Tribune* as "a classic," *The Rise of Theodore Roosevelt* stands as one of the greatest biographies of our time. This carefully documented biography is full of descriptions of Roosevelt's pre-Presidential years, his Presidency, his love of adventure, his family life, his governorship of New York and his writing career.

Muller, Melissa, translated by Rita and Robert Kimber with an Epilogue by Miep Giess. *Anne Frank: The Biography.* This biography tells of the girl whose fate has touched the lives of millions and has become the "human face of the Holocaust." Her diary of 25 months in hiding was a precious record of her struggle to keep hope alive through the darkest days of World War II.

Nagel, Paul C. *John Quincy Adams.* Following in his father's footsteps, John Quincy Adams is reared, educated and groomed to be President. It shows the careful planning that was undertaken to prepare him for the Presidency from the time he was secretary to the Minister of Russia at age 14 to his Presidency.

Nasaw, David. *Chief: The Life of William Randolph Hearst.* This is the biography of one of the most renowned enormous American newspaper publishing moguls, William Randolph Hearst. It includes his connections with Hitler, Mussolini and Churchill, as well as every American President from Grover Cleveland to FDR. Hearst used his media stronghold to gain political power.

Quine, Judith Balaban. *The Bridesmaids.* This biography of 20th century legendary movie actress and Princess of Monaco presents an accurate account of Grace Kelly's life and her marriage to Prince Rainier of Monaco. *The Bridesmaids* presents an intimate picture of her and her life as a glittering celebrity. The biography also reveals a woman of great loyalty and humor living in the world of wealth, splendor, glamour, royal pomp.

Rampersand, Arnold. *Jackie Robinson: A Biography.* The extraordinary life of Jackie Robinson is illuminated in this biography by Arnold Rampersand. We are brought closer to the great ballplayer, a man of courage and quality, who became a pivotal figure in the areas of race relations and civil rights, in addition to being an outstanding athlete.

Read, Nat B. *Don Benito Wilson.* This biography recounts the life of Don Benito Wilson, also known as Benjamin Davis Nelson, a Californian for whom Mount Wilson is named. Few others in California have made such a mark and left such an impact on the state's history as did

Don Benito Wilson. His Wilson College eventually became the present-day University of Southern California.

Rogers, Gary MacLean. *Alexander.* Alexander the Great has been known as not only powerful and legendary, but also mysterious. Who was this man of power? Gary Roger's biography of this great leader reveals the truth about him, a man who was a most imaginative and risk-taking military strategist and a man who grieved because when he was 30 years old, there were no more known worlds to conquer!

Silverstein, Ken. *Radioactive Boy Scout.* While working on his Atomic Energy merit badge for the Boy Scouts, David's obsessive attention turned to nuclear energy, leading him to build a model nuclear breeder reactor in his backyard garden shed. His unsupervised project finally sparks an environmental catastrophe that puts his town's 40,000 residents at risk.

Smith, Sean. *J. K. Rowling: A Biography.* This biography tells about J.K. Rowling, who wrote the Harry Potter novels. A quiet, dreamy, rather shy woman, her brilliance in translating her dreams into prose transforms her own life

St. Johns, Adele Rogers. *Final Verdict.* Adela Rogers St. Johns wrote this biography about her father, Earl Rogers, a renowned Los Angeles criminal attorney. She presents a portrait of him and his unusual clients: celebrities, millionaires, politicians. Readers will gain an insight into the legal system and how cases were won, mainly from the impact of Rogers' words.

Swanson, James L. *Manhunt.* The assassination of Abraham Lincoln resulted in one of the greatest manhunts in the country's history. Swanson's story is a spellbinding hour-by-hour historical chronicle of the pursuit and capture of John Wilkes Booth.

Truman, Margaret. *Bess Truman.* Margaret Truman, daughter of President Harry S. and Bess Truman, pays tribute to her mother in this biography. Margaret Truman writes of the long marriage of her parents and her mother's enduring the difficult political pressures that occurred during Harry Truman's Presidency.

Turner, Pamela. *A Life in the Wild: George Schaller's Struggle to Save the Last Great Beasts.* Pamela Turner's biography of explorer-naturalist George Schaller focuses on his mission: to save the great wild beasts of the world and their surroundings. His insights about species and environment have led him to advocate successfully for the protection of over 190,000 square miles of wilderness around the world.

Wadsworth, Ginger. *First Girl Scout: The Life of Juliette Gordon Low.* This biography is an illustrated account of the life of the woman who founded the Girl Scouts. She witnessed important eras in U.S. history, from the Civil War and Reconstruction to Westward Expansion to post-World War I.

Walls, Jeannette. *Half-Broke Horses.* *Half-Broke Horses* is the story about a young woman and the challenges, setbacks and adventures she faced growing up and living on a Southwest ranch during the early part of the 20th century. The biography about her life as a teacher and ranch owner presents a vivid picture of her life.

White, Ronald C. *Lincoln's Greatest Speech. The Second Inaugural.* On March 4, 1865, Lincoln delivers his Second Inaugural speech. Americans wondered what he would say about the Civil War, about slavery and about Reconstruction. He shared only 703 words and the public was stunned. What did he ask of all Americans?

White, Ronald C. *The Eloquent President: A Portrait of Lincoln Through His Words.* With the outbreak of the Civil War, Lincoln delivered his message to Congress on July 4, 1861. In this text the historian Ronald C. White examines Lincoln's gifts as an orator, communicator and his role as a leader. The author gives insight regarding Lincoln's speeches, the great battles and his private despair

White, Ronald C. *A Lincoln. A Biography.* This is an important biography. Through extensive research utilizing primary resources: letters, photographs and legal papers, the author offers the reader a definition of Lincoln as a man of great integrity.

Wooten, Jim. We Are All the Same: The Story of a Boy's Courage and a Mother's Love. Jim Wooten tells the extraordinary story of the little South African boy whose bravery and fierce determination to make a difference despite being born with AIDS. He becomes a symbol of the world's fight against the disease and has inspired many.

Another Writer's Beginnings...

Genre: Non-Fiction
Biography
Task Two of Three: Reporting Your Findings

During Task One, you read a biography and copied words, phrases and sentences that struck you as important to the biographical sketch.

Your teacher will now designate a day when you are to bring your book and your notes to class. Review your <u>notes</u> carefully. With a partner and using your notes <u>only</u>, tell your partner what you have learned about your subject. Each person will have two to five minutes to share the information.

Another Writer's Beginnings...

A pen to the letter writer is like a brush to the artist.
Alexandra Stoddard
Author, Designer

Genre: Non-Fiction
Biography
Task Three of Three: Writing a Letter – An Artist's Brush

A well-written letter can be gripping. It can spur us to action, provoke us, transform us or even uplift us. Like an intimate conversation, a letter can be written for any reason. It can be as long as needed to complete your purpose in writing it.

Getting Started by Developing the Draft

This task asks you to write a personal letter to the subject of the biography you read. The content of the letter will be based on the notes you prepared for Task One. The following guidelines are suggested:

Paragraph One
Briefly introduce yourself and connect with your subject.

Paragraph Two
From your notes, select a topic, such as a goal, challenge or contribution, to discuss with your subject in your letter,

Paragraph Three
What did you learn from your subject? Did his or her life motivate or uplift you in a positive way? Or, if the subject left you with a negative impression, what was that impression and how did it affect you? Develop with details.

Paragraph Four
Bring your letter to a close in a few sentences.

- You may want to comment on the author's craft in writing the biography.

or

- You may want to reflect on something you found beautiful or disturbing about the subject's life.

Format of a Personal Letter

People write personal letters for various reasons. Regardless of the intent of the letter, it needs to be well organized and well written. A personal letter has its own format. The following guidelines show its basic characteristics:

Heading
- Write your address.
- Write the date.
- Do not include your name in this heading.

Greeting/Salutation
- Open the letter to the subject using the subject's name.
- Begin the greeting with Dear _____.
- Put a comma after the greeting.

Body Paragraphs

- Write the message in the body (paragraphs 1,2,3).
- Draw your letter to a close appropriately in the final body paragraph (paragraph 4), using two or three sentences

Closing

- End your letter with "Sincerely," "Very truly yours" or "Best regards." Be sure a comma follows the closing word or words.

Signature

- Sign your first and last name beneath the closing.

Note: When you turn in your assignment, include the following:

- Task pages
- Your notes
- Final copy of your letter

Another Writer's Beginnings...

Notes to the Teacher

Personal Letter Format

The teacher may choose to do a more detailed review of the format and writing of a personal letter and its proper punctuation.

Assessment

The manner of assessment is left to the discretion of the teacher. However, we suggest that separate grades or scores and comments be given for the three tasks: Reading/Note taking, Reporting and the Personal Letter.

- Content
- Organization
- Mechanics

Chapter 8

A Critic's Eye

A Critic's Eye

*'Tis the good reader that makes the good book; in every
book he finds passages which seem confidences or asides
hidden from all else and unmistakably meant for his ear; . . .*
                                        Ralph Waldo Emerson

Genre: Fiction or Non-fiction
The Book Review

In his role as editor for Charles Scribner's Sons Publishing Company, Maxwell Perkins guided some of the greatest American authors, including F. Scott Fitzgerald, Marjorie Rawlings, Ernest Hemingway, Ring Lardner, Thomas Wolfe and James Jones. He actively sought out promising young writers, and his gift for eliciting their talent is legendary. He helped shape American literature and influenced his successors, who share his belief that "there could be nothing so important as a book can be."

Introduction

Many people love to read! Reading becomes a life-long joy, which rarely flags nor fails. Good writers allow their readers to see life through lenses that magnify and deepen experiences. Whatever they read may trigger remembrances of earlier happenings in their life. They may connect what they read to an outing at the beach, to a house where they once lived, to a serious illness or to one of the most important days in their life. In their search for material to read, they might refer to book reviews. Book reviews help readers decide whether to read a particular book or not, to buy a book or to check it out of the library, depending on the opinions of reviewers.

A book review is a description, a critical analysis and an assessment of a book, whether it is fiction or non-fiction. Book reviews can be found in numerous sources: magazines, newspapers such as the *New York Times, The Los Angeles Times* and *The Wall Street Journal* or on book web sites.

Great Reads
Task One: Selecting a Book

Recommendations have been provided to assist you in selecting a book to read for this assignment. The list includes fiction and non-fiction entries for elementary school, middle school and high school levels. Select a book from the list or one of your own choosing.

Fiction/Science Fiction

A novel isn't a photograph of real life,
it's a commentary on real life.
                                    Richard Peck

- Avi. *Nothing but the Truth*
- Alexander, Lloyd. *Arkadians*
- Ausubel, Ramona. *No One Is Here Except All of Us*
- Broach, Elise. *Fleabrain Loves Franny*
- Chu, Wesley. *The Lives of Tao*
- Cleave, Chris. *Gold*
- Cooney, Caroline. *Among Friends*
- Doerr, Anthony. *All the Light We Cannot See*
- Dolan, Elizabeth. *Elizabeth the First Wife*
- Evans, Paul. *The Last Promise*
- George, Alex. *The Good American*
- Gillham, David R. *City of Women*
- Hautzig, Esther. *The Endless Steppe*
- Hilton, James. *Good-bye, Mr. Chips*
- Hosseini, Khaled. *The Kite Runner*
- Ivey, Eowyn. *The Snow Child*
- Juster, Norton. *The Phantom Tollbooth*
- Kingsolver, Barbara. *Flight Behavior*
- Ludlum, Robert. *The Ambler Warning*
- McMurtry, Larry. *Some Can Whistle*
- Morais, Richard. *The Hundred Foot Journey*
- Naylor, Phyllis Reynolds. *Alice the Brave*
- Orwell, George. *Animal Farm*
- Paterson, Katherine. *Lyddie*
- Paulsen, Gary. *The Haymeadow*
- Plummer, Louise. *The Unlikely Romance of Kate Bjorkman*
- Rylant, Cynthia. *The Van Gogh Café*
- Rogan, Charlotte. *The Lifeboat*
- Smelcer, John. *Edge of Nowhere.*
- Stedman, M.L. *The Light Between Oceans*
- Urrea, Luis Alberto. *The Hummingbird's Daughter*
- White, E.B. *Charlotte's Web*
- Zusak, Markus. *The Book Thief*

Non-Fiction

Inspired, passionate, and specific.
The reader emerges...overjoyed and enlightened.
Julia Cameron

- Asinof, Eliot. *Eight Men Out*
- Astaire, Fred. *Steps in Time: An Autobiography*
- Berg, Scott A. *A Biography of Woodrow Wilson*
- Block, Lawrence. *Step by Step: A Pedestrian Memoir*
- Brown, Daniel James. *The Boys in the Boat*
- Bruchac, Joseph. *A Boy Called Slow: the True Story of Sitting Bull*
- DeFelice, Jim. *Code Name: Johnny Walker: The Extraordinary Story of the Iraqi Who Risked Everything to Fight with the U.S. Navy Seals*
- Duncan, Dayton. *Out West: A Journey Through Lewis & Clark's America*
- Douglas, William O. *Of Men and Mountains: The Classic Memoir of Wilderness*
- Engel, Elliot. *A Dab Of Dickens & A Touch Of Twain*
- Feynman, Richard. *The Pleasure of Finding Things Out*
- Filipovic, Zlata. *Zlata's Diary: A Child's Life in Sarajevo*
- Fritz, Jean. *You Want Women to Vote, Lizzie Stanton?*
- Goodall, Jane. *My Life with the Chimpanzees*
- Grant, Ulysses S. *Personal Memoirs of Ulysses S. Grant*
- Hirschhorn, Clive. *Gene Kelly: A Biography*
- Korda, Michael. *Ike: An American Hero*
- Krauthammer, Charles. *Things That Matter*
- Kuralt, Charles. *Charles Kuralt's America*
- Lindbergh, Anne Morrow. *Gift from the Sea*
- McCullough, David. *Brave Companions: Portraits in History*
- Miller, John. *Darling Judi: A Celebration of Judi Dench*
- Moeller, John. *Dining at the White House: From The President's Table to Yours*
- Moon, William Heath. *Blue Highways*
- Mowat, Farley. *Never Cry Wolf: Amazing True Story of Life Among Arctic Wolves*
- Prager, Dennis. *Happiness Is a Serious Problem*
- Prager, Joshua. *The Echoing Green*
- Roberts, Cokie. *Founding Mothers*
- Saigal, Monique. *French Heroines, 1940-1945 Courage, Strength and Ingenuity*
- Slatkin, Leonard. *Conducting Business: Unveiling the Mystery Behind the Maestro*
- Solomon, Deborah. *American Mirror: A Chronicle of the Life of the Artist, Norman Rockwell*
- Twain, Mark. *Life on the Mississippi*
- White, Ronald C. *American Ulysses: A Life of Ulysses S. Grant*
- Wright, Richard. *Black Boy*

The Book Review
Task Two: Reading and Taking Notes

Having selected your book, take notes while reading to make the final task easier. As you read, make notations of your thoughts, ideas and impressions of what you are reading. This will help in writing your review.

Fiction

If you selected a fiction book, refer to the following suggestions:
- How are the various elements of the plot handled?
- Who are the characters and how are they developed?
- What role does the setting play?
- How realistic is the dialogue?
- What is the theme and how is it revealed?

Non-fiction

If you selected a non-fiction book, refer to the following suggestions:
- What is the subject or genre of the book?
- What is the author's purpose?
- What is the author's premise? Is it to present information to convince the reader to understand and accept his or her viewpoint?
- Who is the intended audience?
- Is the material written with clarity and is it developed fully?

A Critic's Eye

The Book Review
Task Three: Writing the Book Review

As Emerson believed, an insightful reader is able to capture the essence of a book and personalize it. Remember that book reviews are highly personal and reflect the opinions of the reviewer. Your goal, as the critic, is to have the reader value your opinions.

Format of the Review (Fiction and Non-fiction)

List the essential information about the book: title, author, genre, publisher, publishing date and number of pages. To help you with this step, you are encouraged to consult the book section of various newspapers. A model sample is provided below:

American Mirror: The Life and Art of Norman Rockwell
By Deborah Solomon
Non-fiction
Farrar, Straus and Giroux Publishing
Publishing Date: 2013
493 pages

By Jonathan Lopez (writer of the review)

The body of the review is less structured and more insightful. Review your notes to formulate a statement that will describe the book. Include specific evidence from the book. The content of your review will determine the number of paragraphs needed to complete your appraisal.

Introduction to the Written Review (Fiction and Non-fiction)

Begin the review with a catchy phrase, anecdote or quotation that succinctly presents the subject and content of the book. In the next paragraph, focus on a brief summary of the plot if the book is fiction or the purpose of the book if it is non-fiction. Keep the summary brief as analysis takes priority in a book review. Explain how the book affected you.

Analysis and/or Personal Reaction

If the book is fiction, comment on the plot, characters, setting and theme. If the book is non-fiction, state and respond to the central issue of the book and how it is supported. Do not reveal the ending of the novel or the solution to the premise of the non-fiction book. You want the reader to find the answers when he/she reads the book.

Conclusion and Recommendation

State your opinion regarding the book. Assess the book for interest, importance and usefulness. Balance the strengths and the weaknesses in your assessment. This is where you make any comments on the overall value or quality of the book.

Teacher Assessment

An assessment model for both fiction and non-fiction has been designed for the Book Review assignment. The teacher may use one of these model samples or create one of his/her own.

A Critic's Eye
Book Review Assessment
Fiction Book Review
Elementary School, Middle School, High School

Content Criteria		Grade
Purpose	Gives the reviewer's opinion; provides information to help others decide whether or not to read it.	
Introduction/ Beginning	Includes the title, author, genre, publisher, publication date, number of pages; hooks the reader; summarizes the book VERY briefly but does not reveal the ending.	
Body	Includes comments regarding character, theme, setting, plot.	
Conclusion/ Ending	States the assessment and opinion of the novel.	
Composite Grade	Average of the individual grades for each of the above areas	

Mechanics Criteria/Surface Correctness		Grade
Language	Uses words correctly and varies sentence structure	
Surface Correctness	Uses correct spelling, punctuation, capitalization, and grammar	
Composite Grade	Average of the individual grades for each of the above two areas	

Comments:

A Critic's Eye
Book Review Assessment
Non-Fiction Book Review
Elementary School, Middle School, High School

Content Criteria		Grade
Purpose	Gives the reviewer's opinion; provides information to help others decide whether or not to read it.	
Introduction/ Beginning	Includes the title, author, genre, publisher, publication date, number of pages; hooks the reader; VERY briefly summarizes a **few** of the main ideas.	
Body	Explains how well the author achieves his/her purpose; includes a main idea in each paragraph that helps prove the reviewer's point; supports each main idea with evidence from the book.	
Conclusion/ Ending	Reviewer expresses and gives a personal opinion about the book.	
Composite Grade	Average of the individual grades for each of the above areas	

Mechanics Criteria/Surface Correctness		Grade
Language	Uses words correctly and varies sentence structure	
Surface Correctness	Uses correct spelling, punctuation, capitalization, and grammar	
Composite Grade	Average of the individual grades for each of the above two areas	

Comments:

Chapter 9

Story Teller Extraordinaire

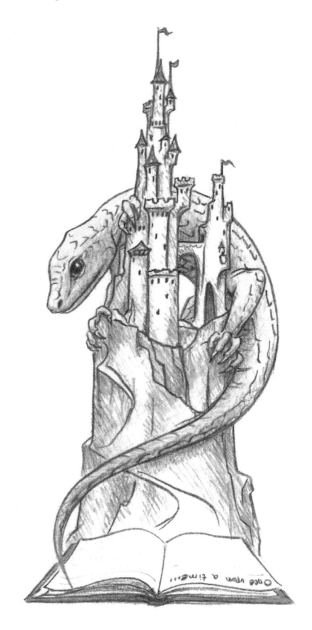

Story Teller Extraordinaire
Once upon a time. . .

*Draw your chair up close to the edge of the precipice
and I'll tell you a story.*

F. Scott Fitzgerald

Genre: Fables, Fairy Tales, Folk Tales, Legends and Myths
Storytelling

Introduction

Everyone has a story to tell – a narrative. It is a way to share and interpret experiences. Storytelling is universal and connects people culturally, no matter the language of origin.

Storytelling predates writing with the earliest forms being oral, combined with gestures. It is an interactive art of presenting events and connects the speaker with the listeners.

Stories include fables, fairy tales, folk tales, legends or myths from past generations that reflect the wisdom and knowledge of early people. These tales are human and reflect a way of thinking, a way of life and a sense of place. Like fiction, the primary elements of storytelling include plot, characters and narrative point of view. Some of the most famous well-known story tellers include the Grimm Brothers, Hans Christian Andersen, Charles Perrault and Scheherazade. Works by Washington Irving and Mark Twain center on characters that are a part of the American culture.

Storytelling is a form of literature that includes the following:

- Fable – A fable is a <u>succinct story</u> which illustrates a particular moral and teaches a lesson to children or has a message as a parable might have. Examples: "The Tortoise and the Hare," "The Lion and the Mouse," "The Fox and the Crow."

- Fairy Tale – A fairy tale is a type of short story that has fairies, goblins, elves, trolls, dwarfs, giants, witches, mermaids or gnomes and usually includes magic or witchcraft. Examples: "Cinderella," "Goldilocks and the Three Bears," "Snow White and the Seven Dwarfs."

- Folk Tale – A folk tale is a fictional story that comes from oral tradition. It is about people or animals dealing with everyday life. Superstitions are important elements in folk tales and folk lore.
  Examples: "Brer Rabbit Falls Down the Well" and "The Birth of Pecos Bill."

- Legend – A legend is a story about superhuman beings such as gods, goddesses and heroes and may explain a cultural practice or natural phenomenon. The legend may have an element of truth. Examples: Robin Hood or King Arthur.

- Myth – A myth is a traditional story which may describe an origin of a group of people or the world. It is an attempt to explain mysterious cultural traditions or supernatural events. Examples: "Phaethon, Son of Apollo" and "Persephone and Demeter."

Task One: Selecting and Reading a Fable, Fairy Tale or Folk Tale
Note: For this assignment, this task focuses primarily on fable, fairy tale and folk tale.

Select and read from the list or one of your own choosing a fable, fairy tale or folk tale. The following list includes the titles, and some have the ***storyteller's original wording*** of the beginnings of the stories to pique your interest. By reading the original wording of the text, you are transformed into the world of the storyteller. Be aware that some of the annotations use the language, dialect and wording of the time. Research several stories available in your local library or on the search engine of your computer. Decide which story appeals to you. If you prefer, you may choose to select one that is familiar and meaningful to you, such as "Goldilocks and the Three Bears," "The Three Little Pigs," "Little Red Riding Hood" or even Oscar Wilde's story "The Selfish Giant."

FABLES

"The Fighting Roosters and the Eagle" by Aesop. Two game roosters were fiercely fighting for the mastery of the farmyard. One at last put the other to flight. The vanquished Rooster skulked away and hid himself in a quiet corner, while the conqueror, flying up to a high wall, flapped his wings and crowed exultingly with all his might. An Eagle sailing through the air pounced upon him and carried him off in his talons. The vanquished Rooster immediately came out of his corner, and ruled henceforth with undisputed mastery.

"The Fox and the Grapes" by Aesop. Driven by hunger, a fox tries to reach some grapes hanging high on the vine but is unable, although he leaped with all his strength. As he goes away, the fox remarks, "Oh, you aren't even ripe yet! I don't need any sour grapes." People who speak disparagingly of things that they cannot attain would do well to apply this story to themselves.

"The Lion and the Beetle" retold by S.E. Schlosser. King Lion goes on a tour in his regal attire to show off what a beautiful and noble creature he is. Everyone on his way bows low to pay him respect. Then, he runs into tiny Beetle. He suspects that Beetle is not bowing to him. He commands Beetle to bow low. Beetle is actually bowing; but from the height from which the King is looking, it seems as though Beetle is not. King bows low himself, so low that he finally loses control.

"The Lion and the Mouse" by Aesop. A lion threatens a mouse that wakes him up. The mouse begs forgiveness and makes the point that such unworthy prey would bring the lion no honor. The lion then agrees and sets the mouse free. Later, the lion is netted by hunters and the lion roars loudly. Hearing the roar, the mouse remembers its clemency and frees the lion by gnawing through the ropes.

FAIRY TALES

"Aladdin and the Wonderful Lamp," an Arabian Nights Fairy Tale. There once lived a poor tailor, who had a son called Aladdin, a careless, idle boy who would do nothing but play ball all day long in the streets with little idle boys like himself. This so grieved the father that he died; yet, in spite of his mother's tears and prayers, Aladdin did not mend his ways.

"The Angel" by Hans Christian Andersen. A child has died, and an angel is escorting him to Heaven. They wander over the earth for a while, visiting well-known places. Along the way they gather flowers to transplant into the gardens of Heaven. The angel takes the child to a poverty-stricken area where a dead field lily lies in a trash heap. The angel salvages the flower explaining that it had cheered a crippled boy before he died. What does the angel reveal?

"Emperor's New Clothes, The" by Hans Christian Andersen. This fairy tale is about two weavers who promise an Emperor a new suit of clothes that is invisible to those unfit for their positions, stupid, or incompetent. When the Emperor parades before his subjects in his new clothes, a child cries out, "But he isn't wearing anything at all!" The tale has been translated into over a hundred languages.

"King of Persia and the Princess of the Sea, The," an Arabian Nights Fairy Tale. There was a King in Persia. He was magnificent, but he had no son. When he was sitting in his court, a merchant came from a far country. He sent the message that he wanted to see him on some important matter. The King ordered his presence. When he came, he said to the King, "Sir, I have a slave who is so beautiful that you will surely marry her." The King ordered him to present her. When the King saw her beauty, he immediately planned to marry her.

"Little Mermaid, The" by Hans Christian Andersen. A young, carefree mermaid named Lena lives a happy life in her home under the sea until, after disobeying her father, she swims to the surface and meets the handsome Prince Stephan. After rescuing her prince from drowning, Lena runs to the aid of the wicked sea-witch Cassandra, who, in exchange for her voice, gives Lena legs to walk on land and the warning that if Prince Stephan were to marry someone else, Lena would then turn forever into sea foam.

"Puss in Boots" by Charles Perrault. A cat uses trickery and deceit to gain power, wealth, and the hand of a princess in marriage for his penniless and low-born master.

"Rapunzel" by the Grimm Brothers. A lonely couple wanted a child and lived next to a walled garden which belonged to a witch. During her pregnancy, the wife notices a Rapunzel plant planted in the garden and longed for it to the point of death. For two nights, the husband went out and broke into the garden to gather some for her; on the third night, as he was scaling the wall to return home, the witch caught him and accused him of theft. He begged for mercy, and the old woman agreed to be lenient, on condition that the then-unborn child be surrendered to her at birth.

"Ugly Duckling, The" by Hans Christian Andersen. A homely little bird is "born" in a barnyard. He suffers abuse from the others around him until, much to his delight and to the surprise of others, a transformation occurs.

FOLK TALES

"Armadillo's Song," a Folk Tale from Bolivia. An armadillo loves music more than anything in the world. After every rainfall, the armadillo would drag his shell to the large pond filled with frogs and he would listen to the big green frogs singing back and forth, back and forth to each other in the most amazing voices.

"Bear Lake Monster," an American Ghost Folk Tale from the State of Utah. If you travel to Bear Lake in Utah on a quiet day, you just might catch a glimpse of the Bear Lake Monster. The monster looks like a huge brown snake and is nearly 90 feet long. It has ears that stick out from the side of its skinny head and a mouth big enough to eat a man. According to some, it has small legs and it kind of scurries when it ventures out on land. But in the water - watch out!

"Bigfoot Wallace and the Hickory Nuts," an American Folk Tale from the State of Texas. Bigfoot Wallace was as crazy an individual as they come. He could spin a yarn better than anyone, and while he was a dangerous foe to his enemies, he was also a jovial giant, who was always on the lookout for a good laugh. What with hunting and fishing and fighting Comanches and avoiding rattlesnakes, Wallace had the time of his life in Texas. Said he wouldn't swap Texas for the whole shooting match that was the rest of the United States.

"Birth of Paul Bunyan," an American Folk Tale from the State of Maine. Now I hear tell that Paul Bunyan was born in Bangor, Maine. It took five giant storks to deliver Paul to his parents. His first bed was a lumber wagon pulled by a team of horses. His father had to drive the wagon up to the top of Maine and back whenever he wanted to rock the baby to sleep...

"Birth of Pecos Bill," an American Folk Tale from the State of Texas. Well now Pecos Bill was born in the usual way to a real nice cowpoke and his wife who were journeying west with their eighteen children. Bill's Ma knew right from the start that he was something else. He started talkin' before he was a month old, did his teething on his Pa's bowie knife and rode his first horse jest as soon as he learned to sit up on his own. When he started to crawl, Pecos Bill would slither out of the wagon while his Mama was cookin' supper and wrestle with the bear cubs and other wild animals that roamed the prairies.

"Brer Rabbit Falls Down the Well," an American Folk Tale from the State of Georgia. One day, Brer Rabbit and Brer Fox and Brer Coon and Brer Bear and a lot of other animals decided to work together to plant a garden full of corn for roasting. They started early in the morning and raked and dug and raked some more, breaking up the hard ground so it would be ready for planting. It was a hot day, and Brer Rabbit got tired mighty quick. But he kept toting off the brush and clearing away the debris 'cause he didn't want anyone to call him lazy.

"Callin' the Dog," an American Folk Tale for the State of Mississippi. Tall talkin' in Mississippi has been termed "Callin' the dog" ever since that famous tall-tale session when one man offered a hound dog pup to the person who could tell the biggest lie. Those stories started rollin' in, each one bigger and harder to believe than the one before.

"Celebrated Jumping Frog of Calaveras County" by Mark Twain. A man from the East comes to a western mining town. At the request of a friend, the narrator speaks with Simon Wheeler in order to ask about a man named Leonidas W. Smiley. Instead of giving the narrator the information that he asks for, Wheeler launches into a tall tale about a man named Jim Smiley. Read how Jim Smiley, who would bet on anything, makes a bet about his pet frog and how that frog became the "Celebrated Jumping Frog of Calaveras County."

"Cowboys in Heaven," an American Folk Tale from the State of Texas. After cow punching for nigh on fifty years, a Texas cowboy went on to his reward. There was considerable excitement in heaven when he reached the pearly gates. The arrival of a real Texan cowboy was considered something of an event in heaven. Saint Peter himself came right over and insisted on giving the cowpoke a tour. Things were right friendly-like until the cowboy spotted half-a-dozen cowpokes staked out like broncos.

"Crow Brings the Daylight," an Inuit Tale. Long, long ago, when the world was still new, the Inuit lived in darkness in their home in the fastness of the north. They had never heard of daylight, and when it was first explained to them by Crow, who traveled back and forth between the northlands and the south, they did not believe him. Today, the Inuit live for half a year in darkness and half a year in daylight and they are always kind to Crow, for it was he who brought them the light.

"The Crows Are in the Corn," an American Folk Tale from the State of Georgia. It happened in Georgia not long ago that a farmer and his wife decided to sleep late, like the rich folk do. It was a beautiful Sunday morning, the kind that brings all God's creatures out to play. But not these farm folk. No, they just slept and slept and slept. The crows were gathered in a large oak tree, having a big morning meeting. They noticed that there was nobody stirring around the house, and that the corn was ripe in the field. So they adjourned their meeting mighty quick and flew over to the field to eat some corn.

"The Death of Pecos Bill," an American Folk Tale from the State of New Mexico. Now, Pecos Bill didn't live forever. Nope, not even Bill could figure out how to do that. Here's how he died. . .

"Drought Buster," an American Folk Tale from the State of Nebraska. Back in the early days, the Plains folk were often in need of a good drought buster during the hot summer months. The sun would shine and shine and the clouds would scuttle right quick over the Plains without dropping rain. One year, it got so bad that Febold Feboldson, that legendary Swede who could bust the driest drought in a day, got annoyed. He liked his fishin', right enough, and there was no fishin' to be had in that drought. So he sat down and thought up a way to bust that there drought.

"The Fisherman and the Bear," an American Folk Tale from the State of Maine. One fine day an old Maine man was fishing and fishing on his favorite lake and catching nary a thing. Finally, he gave up and walked back along the shore to his fishing shack. When he got close to the front door, he saw it was open. Being of a suspicious nature, he walked to the door quietly and looked inside. There was a big black bear. It was just pulling the cork out of his molasses jug with its teeth. The molasses spilled all over the floor and the bear rubbed his paw in it, smearing it all over.

"Freddy's Fabulous Frogs" (a Tongue Twister Tale). Fabian Frogmorton stole Freddy's frog Fats on the Friday of the town of Flowerpot's Fabulous Frogs Contest. Freddy was furious. Fabian Frogmorton had cheated Freddy out of the Fabulous Frog Award last year. Fabian had fed Freddy's frog flies just before the Fast Frog Frolic, the final race in Flowerpot's Fabulous Frogs Contest. Freddy's frog had been too full to frolic, .

"Fur-Bearing Trout," an American Folk Tale from the State of Colorado. Now it happened that there was a mining camp in Colorado where more than an average number of the miners were bald. An enterprising hair tonic salesman from Kentucky decided to take advantage of this golden opportunity, so he made the trip north. It was a rainy summer evening. The salesman was headed towards the mining camp with four bottles of hair tonic under his arm. As he was crossing one of the trout streams which lead to the Arkansas River, the salesman slipped and dropped two bottles of hair tonic into the water.

"Ghost Train," a Canadian Folk Tale from Alberta, Canada. I was a railway fireman back in those days, working on the CPR line in Alberta. I did a hard day's work and earned me a fair wage. I was young then, and my pretty little bride was just setting up housekeeping in the little cottage that was all we could afford. Life was good, and I thought everything would continue rolling along that way.

"Green Lantern," an American Folk tale from the State of Michigan. There once was a lighthouse keeper who had lived on St. Martin's Island with his children, whom he loved dearly. They were all alone there, for the mother had died long before. Wanting the best for his daughter and son, the keeper had insisted that they continue their education, and for this purpose had purchased a small dory for them, which they rowed across to the mainland each day to attend school. One spring after, the children were rowing home from school when they were caught in a sudden squall.

"Heron and the Hummingbird," a Native American Tale (Hitchiti Tribe). Heron and Hummingbird were very good friends, even though one was tall and gangly and awkward and one was small and sleek and fast. They both loved to eat fish. The Hummingbird preferred small fish like minnows and Heron liked the large ones. Read how today the Heron owns all the fish in the rivers and lakes, and the Hummingbird sips from the nectar of the many flowers which he enjoyed so much during the race.

"How the Rainbow Was Made," a Creation Tale from the Ojibwa Nation. One day when the earth was new, Nanabozho looked out the window of his house beside the wide waterfall and realized that all of the flowers in his meadow were exactly the same off-white color. How boring! He decided to make a change, so he gathered up his paints and his paintbrushes and went out to the meadow and began to paint.

"Idaho Potatoes," an American Folk Tale from the State of Idaho. We here in Idaho are right proud of our potatoes. Our fields are so chock full of potatoes that you can hear them grumbling when you stick your ear on the ground. "Roll over, yer crowding me," they say. Potatoes grow bigger in Idaho than anywhere else. Once, a greenhorn asked me for a hundred pounds of potato. I set him straight real fast. I don't believe in cutting into one of my potatoes.

"Jack and the Corn Stalk," an American Folk Tale from the State of Kansas. Once, a Kansas farmer sent his son Jack to check on the growth of the corn in the field. Jack was not a tall lad, so he decided to take a ladder with him. When he found a nice big stalk of corn, he leaned the ladder against it and climbed up until he could reach the first joint. From there, he proceeded to the top of the cornstalk, and looked out over the field. There was enough corn there for a rich harvest.

"King of Sharks," a Folk Tale from the State of Hawaiian. One day, the King of Sharks saw a beautiful girl swimming near the shore. He immediately fell in love with the girl. Transforming himself into a handsome man, he dressed himself in the feathered cape of a chief and followed her to her village.

"Mississippi Mosquitoes," an American Folk Tale from the State of Mississippi. A visitor to Mississippi decided to take a walk along the river in the cool of the evening. His host warned him that the mosquitoes in the area had been acting up lately, tormenting the alligators until they moved down the river. But the visitor just laughed and told his host he wasn't to be put off from his evening constitutional by a few mosquitoes.

"Never Mind Them Watermelons," an American Ghost Folk Tale from the State of Alabama. Well now, old Sam Gibb, he didn't believe in ghosts. Not one bit. Everyone in town knew the old log cabin back in the woods was haunted, but Sam Gibb just laughed whenever folks talked about it. Finally, the blacksmith dared Sam Gibb to spend the night in the haunted log cabin. If he stayed there until dawn, the blacksmith would buy him a whole cartload of watermelons. Sam was delighted. Watermelon was Sam's absolute favorite fruit. He accepted the dare at once, packed some matches and his pipe, and went right over to the log cabin to spend the night.

"Old Man Moses," an American Folk Tale from the State of New Hampshire. It's not hard to catch a meal in New Hampshire, no sir. Take my neighbor, Old Man Moses, who lives down a piece from me. One morning, Old Man Moses went out his kitchen door and found twelve turkeys on his fence. He figured one of them would make a good dinner, but he was afeared that if he went to get his gun, them turkeys would be gone when he returned.

"Paul Bunyan Tames the Whistling River," an American Folk Tale from the State of Michigan. The Whistling River -- so named because twice a day, it reared up to a height of two hundred feet and let loose a whistle that could be heard for over six hundred miles -- was the most ornery river in the U.S. of A. It took a fiendish delight in plaguing the life out of the loggers who worked it. It would tie their logs into knots, flip men into the water then toss them back out onto the banks, and break apart whole rafts of logs as soon as the loggers put them together.

"Pecos Bill Rides a Tornado," an American Folk Tale from the State of Kansas. Now everyone in the West knows that Pecos Bill could ride anything. No bronco could throw him, no sir! Fact is, I only heard of Bill getting' throwed once in his whole career as a cowboy. Yep, it was that time he was up Kansas way and decided to ride him a tornado.

"Rip Van Winkle" by **Washington Irving.** Rip Van Winkle, a lazy man, wanders off one day with his dog Wolf into the Catskill Mountains where he runs into an odd group of drinking men. He drinks some of their mysterious brew and passes out. When he wakes up under a tree, he is

astonished to find that 20 years have passed and things are a lot different. This tale tells how America changed due to the Civil War, only in a different and more subtle way than previously told.

"Sally Ann Thunder Ann Whirlwind Crockett Bests Mike Fink," an American Folk Tale from the State of Tennessee. Davy Crockett done married the prettiest, the sassiest, the toughest gal in the West, don't ya know! Her name was Sally Ann Thunder Ann Whirlwind and she was all that and then some! She was tougher than a grumpy she-bear and faster than a wildcat with his tail on fire and sweeter than honey, so that even hornets would let her use their nest for a Sunday-go-to-Meeting hat.

"Sasquatch," an American Ghost Tale from the State of California. I got up at the crack of dawn and drove to Larry's place to pick him up. We were going hiking along our favorite trail in the back of beyond. It was a sunny day, but not too hot; a perfect day for hiking. Larry and I walked along the rugged path leading into the woods, chatting off and on as the mood struck us...

"The Talking Mule," an American Folk Tale from the State of South Carolina. A farmer owned a mule which he used for work all week. But being a Church-going man, he let the mule rest on Sunday. One Sunday, the farmer had to go to a funeral. So he sent his son to saddle the mule. "Since when do I have to work on Sunday?" asked the mule.

"White Horse," a Canadian Folk Tale from Manitoba, Canada. A Cree chief had a very beautiful daughter who was sought after by many brave warriors. There were two suitors who led the rivalry for her hand, a Cree chief from Lake Winnipegosis and a Sioux chief from Devil's Lake. The girl herself favored the Cree warrior, and when he brought a beautiful white horse from Mexico as a gift for her father...

"Why Lizards Can't Sit," an American Folk Tale from the State of Mississippi. Back in the old days, Brer Lizard was an awful lot like Brer Frog, meaning he could sit upright like a dog. Things were like this for quite a spell. Then one day when they were walking down the road by their swamp, Brer Lizard and Brer Frog spotted some real nice pasture land with a great big pond that was on the far side of a great big fence. Ooo did that land look good. Looked like a great place for Brer Lizard to catch insects and other good food. And Brer Frog wanted a swim in that big ol' pool.

"Why Opossum Has a Bare Tail," a Native American Folk Tale from the Cherokee Nation. One day, Opossum was walking in the woods around sunset when he spied Raccoon. Now Opossum had always admired Raccoon because he had a beautiful tail with rings all around it. So Opossum went up to Raccoon and said: "How did you get those pretty rings on your tail?"

Story Teller Extraordinaire
Once upon a time. . .

Genre: Fables, Fairy Tales and Folk Tales
So. . .What's Your Story?
Task Two: Planning the Presentation

You have selected and read a story of your choice. You are now ready to present your story to an audience.

The following strategies are suggested for your presentation:

- Read the story a few times; then read it aloud. Tell the story to yourself in your own words. Check the original version to note what you may have missed.

- Think about the characters: What do they look like? How do they act? What kind of voices do they have? Are they funny, shy, smart, generous or wicked? This step requires reading not only between the lines but also beyond the lines, which means that the answer is not directly stated but is implied.

- Visualize the setting of the story. When and where does it take place?

- Explore the mood you want to create and the images you want your audience to see. Consider exaggerating small details to enhance the story.

- Think about the plot of the story. Block it out; write the beginning, the middle and the end. Plan the story structure any way you wish. You may want to use 5 x 8 index cards for each section of the story.

- Practice the story until it comes naturally. **There is no substitute for preparation!**

- Tell the story to a family member or friend. Have fun telling the story. If you are having fun, so will your audience. **The listener then becomes the co-creator of the story as they experience it.**

- Present the story to the class **in a 3-5 minute time period.** Realize there is no right or wrong way to tell a story; there is only your way.

Optional Suggestion for the Student

Use of gestures, props or costumes is at your discretion. However, you need to provide your teacher with a list of your props and a description of your costume for approval.

Notes to the Teacher

Remind the students that a good presentation requires that they write out and block the story, make note cards and practice. It is suggested that 5" x 8" file cards be used.

A Student Presentation Rubric is included for your assessment of the presentation or you may design one of your own. It is suggested that a copy of the rubric be provided to the students before their scheduled storytelling.

An additional venue beyond the classroom presentation for the students is at your discretion. Consider inviting parents and outside guest to the presentation.

Student Presentation Rubric

Name_____Title_____Date_____

Criteria	4	3	2	1
Content Introduction, body and conclusion	Knowledgeable of content and includes an engaging introduction, detailed body and memorable conclusion	Knowledgeable of content and includes an introduction, detailed body and conclusion	Somewhat knowledgeable of content and is missing an introduction, body or conclusion	Some content facts seem questionable and is missing an introduction, body and/ or conclusion
Eye Contact	Makes eye contact with everyone in the room	Makes eye contact with most everyone in the room	Makes eye contact with some of the people in the room	Makes very little or no eye contact with people in the room
Volume & Clarity Loudness, articulation and no mumbling	The people in the back can hear the speech very clearly	The speaker mumbles a bit but people in the back can hear most of the speech	The speaker mumbles some and the people in the back can hear parts of the speech	The speaker consistently mumbles so that the people in the back cannot hear the speech
Flow Pauses and verbal fillers: um, uh, er	The speech flows nicely with no pauses or distracting verbal fillers	The speech includes 1-2 pauses and a few verbal fillers	The speech includes some distracting pauses and some verbal fillers	Speech includes several distracting pauses and many verbal fillers
Confidence & Attitude	Speaks with enthusiasm, poise and assurance	Mostly speaks with enthusiasm, poise and Assurance	Speaks with some enthusiasm, poise and assurance	Speaks with little or no enthusiasm, poise and/or assurance
Visual Aid	The visual aid complements the speech and is neat, colorful and creative	The visual aid connects to the speech and is mostly neat, colorful and creative	The visual aid somewhat connects to the speech and is somewhat neat, colorful and creative	The visual aid does not connect to the speech and is messy, lacks color and creativity
Time	Speech is given in the time allotted	Speech is 10% short or over the allotted time	Speech is 20% short or over the allotted time	Speech is 30% short or over the allotted time

Grade: _____

Time Speech Began: _____ Time Speech Ended: _____

Chapter 10

Shakespeare Re-imagined

Shakespeare Re-Imagined
The Curtain Opens

Two stars keep not their motion in one sphere; . . .
Prince Henry
Henry IV, Part I, Act 5, Scene 4

Genre: Drama
English Literature and Shakespearean Drama

Notes to the Teacher

The purpose of these lessons is intended to give the teacher an opportunity to use the information herein for teaching any Shakespeare play, regardless of the grade level.

The goal of this study is to bring Shakespeare out of the world of the Renaissance and into the present. This approach allows for traditional academic study, student performance and opportunities for individual and collaborative work. Best of all, the student has the opportunity to discover that

We are such stuff
As dreams are made on, . . .
Prospero
The Tempest, Act. IV, Scene 1

Shakespeare Re-Imagined
The Curtain Opens

I believe that in a great city, or even in a small city or a village,
a great theater is the outward and visible sign
of an inward and probable culture.
Laurence Olivier, British actor

Genre: Drama
Introductory Activity to Shakespearean Drama
For the Student
Quick Write

Drama presents stories to be performed before an audience. More than any other literary forms, drama portrays real life. Watching a play brings a work to life before our eyes because of its staging. This staging includes acting, costumes, sets, music and sound effects. It not only shows actions in the story but also tells about it. Some plays, for example, elicit laughter; others evoke tears. Some are comic; others, tragic; and still others, a mixture of both.

When we read a play, our minds become theater. We "see" the sets and costumes; we visualize the action. Moreover, we understand the voices of the characters as created by the playwright. Many characters in Shakespeare's plays have contrasting personalities. For example, in *Julius Caesar*, Brutus is logical, a man of reason, whereas Mark Anthony is pretentious, a man of emotion.

As an introduction to your study of Elizabethan drama and William Shakespeare, write quickly for five minutes on all or one of more of the following:

- What do you already know about William Shakespeare?
- With which plays are you familiar?
- Have you ever seen a Shakespeare play performed? If so, briefly describe your experience and your reaction.
- What would you like to learn about Elizabethan drama and William Shakespeare?

In a group of no more than four, share your quick write. Select a recorder to compile and cluster the responses to share with the class.

Shakespeare Re-Imagined
The Curtain Opens

This royal throne of kings,
This scepter'd isle...
This blessed plot, this earth,
This realm, this England.

John of Gaunt
Richard II, Act II, Scene 1

Genre: Drama
English Literature

Introduction: Background

English literature might be more accurately called British literature, for it includes literature from Great Britain, which includes Scotland, Wales and Ireland, as well as England.

As a literary form, English literature, as well as the English language, is essentially divided into three periods:

- **Old English (c. 650-1100)**

Old English literature begins with the epic tale *Beowulf*, the oldest surviving epic in the English language, written about 700 A.D. The tales in the epic are stories and legends of monsters, of descents into the Underworld and of battles with dragons. The following are the opening lines from *Beowulf* written in Old English, followed by its translation:

> *Hwæt! We Gardena in gear-dagum,*
> *þeodcyninga, þrym gefrunon,*
> *hu ða æþelingas ellen fremedon.*

> LO, praise of the prowess of people-kings
> of spear-armed Danes, in days long sped,
> we have heard, and what honor the athelings won!

- **Middle English (c. 1100-1500)**

Middle English, the English of London in the 1300's, includes works by Geoffrey Chaucer, who is often called the father of English poetry.

An example of Middle English are the following lines from the "Prologue" to *The Canterbury Tales* with translation:

> Whan that aprill with his shoures soote
> The droghte of march hath perced to the roote,
> And bathed every veyne in swich licour
> Of which vertu engendred is the flour; . . .

> When April with his showers sweet with fruit
> The drought of March has pierced unto the root
> And bathed each vein with liquor that has power

To generate therein and sire the flower; . . .

- **Modern English (c. 1500-present)**

Modern English evolved during the Renaissance Period, specifically during the reign of Elizabeth I. It is an early form of the language we speak today. Some historians date Early Modern English from 1500-1800 and add Late Modern English from 1800 to the present.

The Renaissance and the Renaissance Theater (1485-1660)

Scholars believe that the English had been writing and performing plays before the Renaissance. They speculate that medieval drama evolved from church ceremonies. Dramatic presentations then moved out of the churches into royal palaces, noblemen's homes and eventually into the center of towns. Guilds, the first loosely organized groups that eventually became trade unions, assisted and presented plays that dramatized the history of mankind through Biblical stories.

The word "renaissance" means "rebirth," which refers to a renewed interest in Classical Greek and Roman arts and sciences. Beginning in the early 1500s, a new type of play evolved called the "Interlude." These were one-act plays, some of which were lessons in morality, while others were rowdy farces.

William Shakespeare (1564-1616)

"He was not of an age but for all time."

Ben Johnson

William Shakespeare was born in 1564 in Stratford-upon-Avon, a town northwest of London. His childhood education focused on the classics, such as Plutarch. In school, he read stories of the ancient Greeks and Romans, upon which one of his plays, *Julius Caesar, is based.* In addition, his environment in Stratford provided a rich background for creating characters in his plays. The town was a thriving place of commerce, allowing Shakespeare the chance to meet many different types of people.

As a prolific writer, Shakespeare authored 37 plays, consisting of histories, comedies and tragedies. His more well-known histories include *Richard II, Richard III* and *Henry VIII;* his comedies, *The Taming of the Shrew, Merchant of Venice* and *As You Like It;* his tragedies, *Romeo and Juliet, Julius Caesar, Hamlet, Macbeth* and *Othello.* These plays, along with his 154 sonnets, secured his immortality as the leading playwright and very probably the greatest writer in Western civilization.

Shakespeare was a member of the Lord Chamberlain's Men, an acting company, and helped finance the building of The Globe Theater, where his plays helped the company become successful. In the production of *Henry V,* Shakespeare refers to The Globe in the "Prologue":

A kingdom for a stage, princes to act

And monarchs to behold the swelling scene!. . .

After Queen Elizabeth's death in 1603, James VI of Scotland succeeded her, becoming King James I of Britain, and renamed the acting company The King's Men.

The Globe Theater or "The Wooden O"

By the end of the sixteenth century, theaters were built to provide permanent housing for the plays. The most famous theater was The Globe, built in 1599 along the Thames River in a small town outside London called Southwark. The theater was designed in the shape of a sixteen-sided wooden polygon, giving it a circular appearance, which Shakespeare called "The Wooden O." It was built around the center of a courtyard where plays were performed in the open air on a platform stage. The stage jutted out into the courtyard where the poorer patrons, known as groundlings, stood. The theater also had covered galleries where the wealthy patrons sat.

When a play was to be staged, a white flag was hoisted above the theater. Since natural light was needed, the plays began at 2:00 p.m., a practice which gave rise to our present-day afternoon matinee.

Admission to the theater was open to everyone, regardless of rank or economic status. Groundlings, named after a type of fish that lives on the bottom of lakes and streams, paid a penny and stood on the ground before the stage while those who could afford a more comfortable seating sat in the galleries. The most expensive seats were those on both sides of the stage itself. These were usually reserved for patrons of the theater who rented them. As many as 2000 or more people could attend a play.

In the chapter titled "Shakespeare" in his book *A Dab of Dickens and a Touch of Twain; Literary Lives from Shakespeare's Old England to Frost's New England,* Professor Elliot Engel describes some of the experiences a typical theatergoer would have had in Shakespeare's day.

For admission to the theater, patrons placed their admission fee into a little locked metal box called the "money box." Each time the small money box filled up, the usher took it to a locked office backstage, grabbed an empty box and returned to collect more money. That backstage office became known as the "box office," which evolved into our present-day box office, located at the entrance to the theater.

During Shakespeare's time, actors were highly trained. They were required to memorize lines, dance, sing, fence, wrestle, clown, cry, roar or even whisper and convey subtle messages with gestures or minor changes in their voices. They worked in close proximity to the audience. If the audience disapproved of the play or the actors, they demonstrated their displeasure by jeering and throwing food, which they might have purchased at a refreshment stand inside the theater.

A superstition associated with actors and acting developed at this time. Before an actor performed, someone might encourage the actor to perform so well that the groundlings would drool onto the stage, causing the actor to slip and break a leg. This situation resulted in the present-day custom of saying "break a leg" instead of "good luck" to an actor before he or she begins a performance.

Shakespeare knew his audience well. He was a keen judge of the royal mind and knew what he could say in his plays without drawing the wrath of the nobility. He also knew what the groundlings wanted. He wrote exciting stories with fast-paced, complicated plots with many characters and with poetic imaging to maintain audience interest. In addition, he enriched his productions with elaborate costumes, music and minimal scenery.

Because of the rowdiness of the audience, actors became regarded as vagrants, rogues or other undesirable characters. This unfortunate development resulted in the theater's being identified as scandalous. For that reason, women were not allowed to perform. Thus, the acting companies were comprised only of men and of young boys who played the female roles.

A detailed drawing of the Globe Theatre appears on the next page.

Shakespeare's Histories

Shakespeare's histories are based largely on real historical figures, including Julius Caesar, Antony and Cleopatra, King Lear, Macbeth, King Henry V, King Henry VIII and Richard III. The histories illustrate the moral lessons to be learned from the crimes, activities and often the ambitions of leaders of state.

The main characteristics of a Shakespearean history include the following:

- They are based on the history of England, though with some historical inaccuracies.
- They are not written in chronological historical order.
- They focus on English monarchs.
- They are inspired by patriotism.
- They are centered on the dangers of civil war, issues of royal succession and the decline of the medieval system.
- They ended in catastrophe or in triumph achieved at a price.

Shakespeare's Comedies

A comedy is a play that celebrates and affirms life. Most of the comedies are romantic fantasies, designed to entertain and please the audiences. They are generally festive and joyous and make fun of human foibles. A Shakespearean comedy, by definition, ends happily, often in a marriage.

The main characteristics of a Shakespearean comedy include the following:

- Women share with men the role of dramatic protagonist.
- Young lovers struggle to overcome problems, often the result of interfering elders.
- The young lovers experience separation and reunification.
- There are many mistaken identities, usually the result of disguises.
- Puns and other elements of comedy are used frequently.
- There is a clever servant.
- Family tensions are usually resolved at the end of the play.

Shakespeare's Tragedies

A tragedy highlights life's sorrows, and the main character experiences a great misfortune. The tragedies deal with death, morality and destruction and show how the breaking of a moral law inevitably leads to disaster.

The characteristics of a Shakespearean tragedy include the following:

- The tragic hero, the main character, is generally a person of importance.
- The tragic hero not only has extraordinary abilities but also possesses a tragic flaw, which causes him or her to make an error in judgment or to exhibit a weakness in character that leads to his or her downfall.
- Forces and influences outside the control of the hero contribute to his or her downfall and death.
- Recognizing his or her tragic flaw, the hero gains the audience's sympathy at the play's end.
- The tragic hero comes to an unhappy and miserable end with courage and dignity.

Elements of the Shakespearean Drama

Shakespeare, among others, employed useful devices to reveal to the audience the character's thoughts and feelings. These devices are as follow:

- Soliloquy. This literary device is a meditative speech in which the character is alone on stage and reveals aloud his inner thoughts, pretending that the audience is not present.

    Example: Hamlet's "To be, or not to be..." soliloquy in *Hamlet,* Act III, Scene 1, in which he tells the audience he is contemplating suicide.

- Aside. This device is a character's private, quiet comments about what is happening at that time in the play or about another character. They are spoken "out the side" of his mouth or "under his breath" only for the audience to hear. They are short but just as truthful as the soliloquy. When the line or lines are an "Aside," the word is placed in brackets

    Example:

    CASSIO: This is the monkey's own giving out: she is persuaded I will marry her, out of her own love and clattery, not out of my promise.

    OTHELLO: [Aside.] Iago beckons me; now he begins the story.

    Othello, Act IV, Scene 3

- Poetic Imagery. This device reminds the reader that the play is an unrhymed iambic pentameter poem. Thus, poetry enhances the imagery of the play as singing enhances the opera.

  Example:

  MACBETH: Out, out, brief candle!
  Life's but a walking shadow, a poor player,
  That struts and frets his hour upon the stage,
  And then is heard no more.

  Macbeth, Act V, Scene 5

- Dramatic Irony. Dramatic irony is a contrast between what a character knows and what the reader or audience knows.

  Example: In *Romeo and Juliet*, Act IV, Scene 4, the Capulets are preparing for Juliet's wedding to Paris. Here, the excitement of the Capulet household preparing for the wedding contrasts sharply with the desperation of Juliet's taking the sleeping potion.

Elements of Shakespearean Language

The Shakespearean style of writing created poetic and dramatic images to emphasize a word or to give a character a specific speech pattern. Some of these elements are as follows:

- Contractions and Omissions. Like English spoken today, Shakespeare used many contractions and omissions, but he used them differently. He would contract pronouns that began with vowels. For example: ope ~ open, o'er ~ over, i' ~ in, e'er ~ ever, oft ~ often, e'en ~ even. Moreover, he frequently omitted the unstressed syllable from the middle of a word. For example: "fam'ly" for "family." Today, we use a single pronoun for the people we address "you," whereas Shakespeare had a choice: "thou," "thee," "thy," "thine."

- Puns. Shakespeare had fun with the language. He enjoyed jokes and phrases that had more than one meaning and included them to please his audience. Shakespeare's word play included puns, which are plays on words. For example, in the beginning of *Julius Caesar,* a shoemaker mocks a government official by answering his questions in riddles. When asked what work he does, the shoemaker responds with "I mend bad soles" (Act I, Scene 1).

- Figures of Speech. Shakespeare's rich language often results from his use of figures of speech, including the following from *Julius Caesar*:

  1. Simile: the comparison of two unlike things, using "like" or "as"
     Example:
     His countenance, like richest alchemy [gold] will change to virtue and to worthiness.

  2. Metaphor: the comparison of two unlike things, not using "like" or "as"
     Example:
     You blocks, you stones, you worse than senseless things!

  3. Hyperbole: a highly-exaggerated figure of speech
     Example:
     And when you saw his [Pompey's] chariot but appear,
     have you not made an universal shout, that Tiber
     trembled underneath her banks to hear the replication of

your sounds safe in her concave shores?

4. Personification: giving human characteristics to a concept or inanimate   object
Example:

Danger knows full well that Caesar is more dangerous than he.

Shakespeare is credited with inventing new words and creating numerous expressions and sayings that are in use today. Some of those expressions include the following: *break the ice; in my heart of hearts; all that glisters* [glitters] *is not gold; it's a wise father that knows his own child; neither a borrower nor a lender be; knock, knock! Who's there?; in a pickle; wear my heart upon my sleeve; laughing stock; and last but not least; good riddance.* Thus, it is easy understand why his language is our language today.

Shakespeare Re-Imagined
The Curtain Opens

Give every man thy
ear, but few thy voice.
Prince Hamlet
Hamlet, Prince of Denmark
Act I, Scene 3

Genre: Drama
Shakespearean Drama
Task Two: Weaving the Past into the Present

Writing Your Soliloquy

A soliloquy is a meditative speech in which the character is alone on stage and reveals aloud his inner thoughts, pretending that the audience is not present.

Begin writing in class a draft of a brief soliloquy either in prose or imitating Shakespeare's blank verse about your own personal inner thoughts on any appropriate subject. The final edited copy to be turned in to the teacher may be completed at home.

In writing your soliloquy, consider the following:

- Decide and focus on *one specific* situation. **Think small.**
- Review and understand the incident and the situation that is the subject of your soliloquy.
- Write down quickly your thoughts and the feelings they convey.
- Revise and finalize your soliloquy to be sure it is in harmony with Shakespeare's style, whether prose or blank verse.

Sharing Your Soliloquy

In groups consisting of 3 or 4 students, each student will read his or her soliloquy. The group will respond to each reading and select one to represent the group for reading to the entire class. The written soliloquies will be submitted to the teacher for assessment.

Assessment

The manner of assessment is left to the discretion of the teacher. A letter grade may be given for content and one for mechanics for each soliloquy. Comments are encouraged. Consider awarding Certificates of Achievement to the top three written soliloquies according to 1st place, 2nd place and 3rd place.

Shakespeare Re-Imagined
The Curtain Opens

All the world's a stage,
And all the men and women merely players:
They have their exits and their entrances;
And one man in his time plays many parts,
Jacques
As You Like It
Act II, Scene 7

Genre: Drama
Shakespearean Drama
Task Three: Performing in an Actor's Workshop

Come, let us to the banquet.
Don John
Much Ado About Nothing, Act II, Scene 1

You have just finished reading a play by William Shakespeare. Now, you have the opportunity to perform a scene from the play. The class will divide itself into groups. How many groups depends on class size and teacher's choice. Once the groups are arranged, collectively choose the act and scene from the play you wish to perform. Prior to the group's performance, the teacher will distribute the assessment criteria.

Preparing the Group Presentation

- Decide on a company name reflective of the Elizabethan period.
- Select a group member to act as facilitator.
- Analyze collectively the scene and determine how to stage it.
- Be sure you understand what has happened immediately before the scene.
- Assign acting roles to be performed by each member.
- Memorize your part, if possible.
- Become the character emotionally.
- Act and say the words at the same time; move as required by the staging.
- Include costumes, props and music if desired and with teacher's approval.
- Rehearse both in and out of class, if possible.

Performing the Group Presentation

- Announce the play and set the scene for your audience.
- Be sure you know how to pronounce unfamiliar words.
- Use your own feelings and thoughts.
- **Speak in a strong voice,** as a strong voice is a vital component of the actor's craft.
- Move as required by the staging.

Shakespeare Re-Imagined
The Curtain Opens

Now bid me run
And I will strive with things impossible; . . .
Ligarius
Julius Caesar
Act II, Scene 1

Genre: Drama
Shakespearean Drama
Performance Assessment

Each student's performance of the scene will be evaluated according to the following criteria:

Grade A Performance

- Student knows his/her part and gives an outstanding delivery.
- Student places proper intonation on key words.
- Student projects voice appropriately.
- Student includes gestures.
- Student appears at ease before the audience.

Grade B Performance

- Student knows his/her part and gives a good delivery.
- Student is articulate.
- Student projects voice adequately.
- Student includes a few gestures.
- Student generally appears at ease before the audience.

Grade C Performance

- Student knows most of his/her part and gives a fair delivery.
- Student needs to emphasize key words or lines.
- Student needs to work on voice projection.
- Student needs to include gestures.
- Student appears somewhat at ease before the audience.

Grade D Performance

- Student knows little of his/her part.
- Student gives a monotone delivery.
- Student does not project voice.
- Student includes a few gestures.
- Student is uncomfortable before the audience.

Shakespeare Re-Imagined
The Curtain Opens

There's a divinity that shapes our ends,
Rough-hew them how we will--
Hamlet
Hamlet, Prince of Denmark, Act II, Scene 2

Genre: Drama
Shakespearean Drama
Task Four (Optional Collaborative Activity): Writing a 16ᵗʰ Century Diary

Scholars often mention Shakespeare's "lost years," from 1581-1691 (ages 17-27) for very little is actually known about his life. They have yet to uncover the drafts of his plays, records of his daily life or his love letters. His life continues to be a mystery even today. Imagine what Shakespeare's personal diary might have looked like if you had an opportunity to read it.

Creating a Diary

This task will require not only class time work but also research at home or at school.

The class will divide itself into groups. How many groups depends on class size and teacher's choice. Based upon your research, collectively create a sample diary entry that might have appeared in Shakespeare's diary during his time. Use the following title format as a guide for the completion of the task:

Personal Diary of
William Shakespeare
Things To Do
in the Year of Our Lord 1601

Brainstorm and compile a list of **at least** 10 "things to do" for your group diary for any date and year during Shakespeare's life. You are encouraged to be creative and imaginative as possible, knowing that there are no "right answers," **except that the entries must coincide with the historical period**.

The following are samples of possible entries:

- Write formal invitation to Her Royal Majesty to the opening of *Hamlet, Prince of Denmark.*
- Make arrangements for father's funeral.
- Meet with clothier for final fitting of opening night attire for *Hamlet*
- Attend dress rehearsal of *Hamlet.*
- Save money to buy more land in Stratford.
- Meet Richard Burbage at the theater.
- Jot down jokes heard last night at the inn.
- Work on draft of new play *Twelfth Night.*

Upon completion of the task, each group will share its diary with the class and receive feedback. Each presentation will be judged on creativity, originality and reflection of the Elizabethan Period.

Any further assessment for this task is left to the discretion of the teacher.

Shakespearean Festivals

Note: To find productions of Shakespeare plays at theaters around the globe, see www.shakespeareforalltime.com/840-2.

The following are the better-known festivals celebrated each year with different plays produced:

Cambridge Shakespeare Festival, Cambridge, England. Open Hand Productions, South Lodge, Thornton Common Road, Thornton Hough, Wirral, CH63 4JU **Tel:** 07955 218824. **Email:** mail@cambridgeshakespeare.com. The Festival stages plays in Cambridge college gardens throughout the summer. Prior to the evening's performance, members of the audience can picnic in this idyllic setting, before sitting back to enjoy an evening of dynamic and highly visual theatre.

World Shakespeare Festival, The Festival is produced by the Royal Shakespeare Company and is reported to be the biggest Shakespeare celebration. The venues for these events are held are across the UK in various locations, including Stratford-upon-Avon, London, Newcastle, Gateshead, Birmingham, South Wales, Brighton, Edinburgh and Vale of Glamorgan. Information and tickets for the festival are available through local travel agents. For a schedule of the plays being presented, see www.journeymart.com.

Shakespeare's Globe Theater, 21 New Globe Walk, Bankside, London SE1 9DT. General inquiries: Phone: +44 (0)20 7902 1400 or at info@shakespearesglobe.com. Website: www.shakespearesglobe.com. Founded by the pioneering American actor and director Sam Wanamaker, Shakespeare's Globe is a unique international resource dedicated to the exploration of Shakespeare's work and the playhouse for which he wrote, through the connected means of performance and education. It stands a few hundred yards from its original site. Together, the Globe Theatre, Globe Exhibition & Tour and Globe Education seek to further the experience and international understanding of Shakespeare in performance. See the website for detailed information about plays and many features of the theater.

The Old Globe, San Diego Shakespeare Festival, Balboa Park, San Diego, California. The internationally acclaimed, Tony Award® -winning Old Globe is one of the most esteemed regional theaters in the country. Shakespearean productions are staged in the outdoor Lowell Davies Festival Theatre, Tuesday through Sunday at 8:00 p.m. For a list of plays, information and tickets, call (619) 234-5623. Website: www.oldglobe.org.

Oregon Shakespeare Festival, 15 S. Pioneer Street, P.O. Box 158, Ashland, Oregon 97520. Phone: 541-482-4331. Toll-Free: 800-219-8161. Email address: boxoffice@osfashland.org. OSF offers not only a number of plays, but also backstage tours, park talks, lectures, classes, workshops, pre- and post-show conversations.

A Selected Bibliography

Applebee, Arthur, et al. *The Language of Literature: British Literature*. Evanston: McDougal   Littell Publishing Company, 2002.

Asimov, Isaac. *Asimov's Guide to Shakespeare*. New York: Avenel Books, 1978.

Burton, Philip. *The Sole Voice, Character Portraits from Shakespeare*. New York: The Dial Press, 1970.

Carlsen, Robert and Miriam Gilbert. *British and Western Literature, A Thematic Approach*.   New York: McGraw Hill Inc., 1985.

Chute, Marchette. *Shakespeare of London*. New York: E.P. Dutton, 1963.

Daniel, Kathleen, et al. *Elements of Literature, Sixth Course: Literature of Britain*. Austin: Holt, Rinehart and Winston, 1997.

Dunton, Downer and Leslie and Alan Riding. *Essential Shakespeare Handbook*. New York: DK Publishing, Inc., 2004.

Engel, Elliot. A *Dab of Dickens & a Touch of Twain, Literary Lives from Shakespeare's Old England to Frost's New England*. New York: Pocket Books, 2002.

Hales, Mick. *Shakespeare in the Garden*. New York: harry n. abrams, Inc., 2006.

Jago, Martin. *To Play or not to Play*, 50 Games for Acting Shakespeare. nc: np, nd.

Kearns, George. *Appreciating Literature*. New York: Macmillan Publishing Company, 1984.

Kearns, George, et al. *English and Western Literature*. New York: Macmillan Publishing Company, 1984.

Krull, Kathleen. *Lives of the Writers, Comedies, Tragedies (and What the Neighbors Thought)*. San Diego: Harcourt Brace & Company, 1994.

Langley, Andrew. Illustrated by June Everett. *Shakespeare's Theatre*. New York: Oxford University Press, 1999.

LaRocco, Christine B. and Elaine B. Johnson. *British & World Literature for Life and Work*. Cincinnati: South-Western Educational Publishing, 1997.

Martin, Reed and Austin Tichenor. *Reduced Shakespeare, The Complete Guide for the Attention Impaired*. New York: Hyperion, 2006.

Matterson, T. M. *The Complete Works of William Shakespeare*. Cleveland: The World Publishing Company, nd.

McCaughrean, Geraldine. *Stories from Shakespeare.* New York: Margaret K. McElderry Books, 1995.
Pollinger, Gina. *A Treasury of Shakespeare's Verse.* New York: Kingfisher, 1995.

Talbott, Frederick. *Shakespeare on Leadership, Timeless Wisdom for Daily Challenges.* Nashville: Thomas Publishing Company, 1994.

Chapter 11

Victorian Writers Who Had Great Expectations

Victorian Literature
Writers Who Had Great Expectations

Genre: Victorian Drama and Novel

Notes to the Teacher

If we want students to think substantively and to develop as readers and writers, we need to give them quality literature. It is the classics as well as the gifted Victorian writers such as the Bronte sisters, Lewis Carroll, Charles Dickens and Robert Louis Stevenson that offer students a variety of ideas and perspectives to stretch their thinking. Classics remove students from the realm of textbooks and challenge them to think about excellence in literature, in writing and in the use of language. A novel such as Robert Louis Stevenson's *Treasure Island* not only can be read on one level as a story but also can lure the reader to a higher form of understanding of life. Novels from the Bronte sisters examine class, myth and gothic themes and the ever-changing role of women. Dickens' novels tend to be portraits of difficult lives in which hard work and perseverance triumph in the end. While reading Lewis Carroll's *Alice in Wonderland,* the student is exposed to rich vocabulary and the motivation and imagination of this complex author.

The first task for students is based on Charles Dickens' *A Christmas Carol.* Israel Horovitz adapted Charles Dickens' novel *A Christmas Carol* into a two-act drama. It is found in many literature anthologies, one being Prentice-Hall, or it can be downloaded on your computer. The work may also be purchased from Dramatists Play Services, Inc. Furthermore, the length of time needed for reading the play out loud and completing the tasks is left to the discretion of the teacher.

Victorian Literature
Writers Who Had Great Expectations

It was the best of times, it was the worst of times,
it was the age of wisdom, it was the age of foolishness,
it was the epoch of belief, it was the epoch of incredulity, it was
the season of Light, it was the season of Darkness, it was the spring
of hope, it was the winter of despair...

A Tale of Two Cities
Charles Dickens

Genre: Victorian Literature

Introduction

The literature of the Victorian Era refers to the works that were written during the reign of Queen Victoria, 1837-1901. This was the age of the English novel when reading novels became a popular pastime. Below are a few noteworthy characteristics of literature of this period:

- Develops complex plots with numerous characters.
- Reflects realistic daily life.
- Incorporates belief in the supernatural.
- Reclaims past chivalry.
- Presents practical problems: reform movements, women's rights, child labor, evolution and political commentary.
- Incorporates medical and scientific advancements, political satire, violence and murder.
- Focuses on moral purposes and ideas of truth, justice, brotherhood and love.
- Seeks profit through writing long novels

For the tasks in this project, you will be reading the play *A Christmas Carol* by Charles Dickens and a novel of your choice from the Victorian period.

Victorian Literature
Writers Who Had Great Expectations

The stage is a magic circle
where only the most real things happen.
P. S. Baber

Genre: Victorian Literature
Guide for Reading Drama

A play is a story with the same elements as fiction (plot, conflict, climax, resolution) characters, setting and theme. Why is a play different? A play relies heavily on dialogue and stage directions.

The following strategies for reading a drama are suggested:
- Read stage directions carefully, noting what is happening in each scene.
- Become familiar with the characters through dialogue, through the characters' own words and through what others say to or about them.
- Make predictions about the characters, about the action and about the outcome.
- Become the character in the play, bringing to it your own interpretation.
- Project your voice.

"A Christmas Carol: Scrooge and Marley"
by Israel Horovitz
from *A Christmas Carol* by Charles Dickens

Task One: Reading the Play Aloud
"A Christmas Carol: Scrooge and Marley"

About the Play

A Christmas Carol is set in 19th century England, a time of rapid industrial growth. The wealthy lived in luxury, but the working poor suffered. Dickens' empathy for the poor is evident in *A Christmas Carol*.

The play opens with the protagonist Ebenezer Scrooge working in his office late on Christmas Eve when his nephew Fred visits to invite him to Christmas dinner. Scrooge declines the invitation with a rant against the holiday and those who celebrate it. As the plot develops and because of his attitude, the reader begins to wonder and question what will happen to Scrooge.

About the Author

Charles Dickens (1812-1870) was born in Portsmouth, England. At the age of 12, he left school to work in a boot-blacking factory because his family was forced to live in debtor's prison. Consequently, he experienced an impoverished childhood, which affected him deeply. "No words can express the secret agony of my soul. . .that I suffered in secret, and that I suffered exquisitely, no one even knew but I." Thus, Dickens own words reveal his brush with hard times and poverty.

Even though his father was released from debtor's prison, Dickens received little formal education. He compensated for it by becoming an avid reader. He was influenced by the stories he read and also by his occasional visits to the theater.

Years later, Dickens began to make up stories about people he observed. He sent the stories to the *Monthly Magazine* under the penname Boz, a family baby name he borrowed from his younger brother. His stories became popular and were published in a book called *Sketches by Boz*. He was now an author! Soon thereafter, he wrote a book in serialized form titled *The Pickwick Papers* about a group of wealthy old gentlemen experiencing a sequence of loosely related adventures. In 1836, the book became a national mania with memorable characters who were portrayed comically, often with exaggerated personality traits. This made him wildly famous and wealthy when he was only 25 years old.

With the publishing of *The Pickwick Papers* an instant success, Dickens was catapulted into fame. His novels were published in monthly installments and later reprinted in book form. These installments made the stories inexpensive and accessible, not only to the middle class but also to the poor, creating a new class of readers. Through this episodic writing, he was able to revise subsequent installments based on the feedback and criticism of his friends and his readers. Each installment left the reader at a crucial point with the hero or heroine in need of help, which became known as the "cliff hanger." This made his readers anxious to read the next installment, which eventually evolved into the modern day "soap opera." In addition, to keep the cost reasonable and to maintain their accessibility to the public, he created, in essence, the paperback book.

Why has Dickens remained so popular? Why is he still read today? Numerous scholars have researched and have written about him, among them Dr. Elliot Engel. He asserts, "What truly gives Charles Dickens his immortality. . . rests on the inimitable characters he created in his novels." He continues, "Ultimately, the secret of Charles Dickens is that his characters will live forever because they never lived in the first place. They were not real when he invented them and they are not real today." He concludes, "...his characters represent unchanging human emotion and feeling" and can't be dated. Some of these characters include, for example, Scrooge and Tiny Tim from *A Christmas Carol* and Miss Havisham from *Great Expectations*.

Why do we still enjoy *A Christmas Carol* each year? Many critics have argued that it remains the "greatest expression of the Christmas spirit in the English language." We still appreciate Dickens' genius because he was successful as a writer, an actor and a social reformer.

Victorian Literature
Writers Who Had Great Expectations

. . .my spirit never walked beyond our
counting-house - mark me! - in life my
spirit never roved beyond the narrow
limits of our money-changing hole;
and weary journeys lie before me!
Marley's Ghost, Act I, scene 111
A Christmas Carol
Charles Dickens

Genre: Victorian Literature
Symbols
Task Two: Connecting the Character with the Theme

Symbols: A symbol is a person, place or thing that, in addition to its literal meaning, has other associations.

Because the character of Scrooge is central to the play, your understanding of why he changes will reveal the theme. The teacher has provided you with an outline drawing of a head. Draw a vertical line down the middle of the face. Label the left side "Scrooge at the Beginning" and the right side "Scrooge at the End." On each side, draw concrete symbols, images, phrases or a combination of these that represent Scrooge's attitude and character at the beginning of the play and the change at the end.

Suggestions for completing the task:

- Use 80-90% of the space.
- Use color markers or colored pencils or. . .
- Use computer graphics.

Victorian Literature
Writers Who Had Great Expectations

SYMBOLS FOR SCROOGE
A Christmas Carol: Scrooge and Marley

Victorian Literature
Writers Who Had Great Expectations

Symbols: Connecting the Character with the Theme
Assessment

In evaluating this assignment, a holistic approach is one option. To earn a grade of "A," the student has completed all of the following:

- Follows directions for the task.
- Uses examples of images, concrete symbols and phrases to represent Scrooge and the theme.
- Demonstrates originality and creativity.

A grade of "B," "C" or "D" indicates that the final product is not as fully developed. We suggest including written teacher comments.

Encourage students to share their work!

Victorian Literature
Writers Who Had Great Expectations

God bless us, every one!
> *Tiny Tim, Act II. Scene v*
> *A Christmas Carol*
> *Charles Dickens*

Genre: Victorian Literature
Task Three: Performing Act II, Scene 5

Notes to the Teacher

The number of groups and how they are arranged is left to the discretion of the teacher. Class time needs to be scheduled for students to block out the Act and Scene and to practice their lines. The students may choose to select someone from the group to act as director and someone to act as facilitator, a person who organizes the group. They may use props, costumes, scenery, with teacher approval. On the designated day, each group will perform Scene 5. Anticipate 3 or 4 days for completion of this task. After the completion of the presentations, allot time for critiquing.

Assessment

In lieu of a letter grade for assessment, awards can be designed and presented. These awards can be determined by the teacher or by an outside person.

Victorian Literature
Writers Who Had Great Expectations

. . .I had sent my heroine straight down a rabbit hole,
to begin with, without the least idea what was to happen afterwards. . .
Lewis Carroll about Alice in Wonderland

Genre: Victorian Literature
Task Four: Selecting a Novel

For Task 4, you are asked to select and read a novel that represents literature written during Queen Victoria's reign. You may select one from the list below or one of your own choosing.

Bronte, Anne	*Agnes Grey*
	The Tenant of Wildfell Hall
Bronte, Charlotte	*Jane Eyre*
	Villette
Bronte, Emily	*Wuthering Heights*
Carroll, Lewis	*Alice in Wonderland*
	Alice Through the Looking Glass
Dickens, Charles	*Pickwick Papers*
	Oliver Twist
	The Old Curiosity Shop
	David Copperfield
	A Tale of Two Cities
	Great Expectations
Doyle, Sir Arthur Conan	*A Study in Scarlet*
	The Sign of Four
Elliot, George	*Silas Marner*
	Middlemarch
Hardy, Thomas	*Far from the Madding Crowd*
	Tess of the d'Urbervilles
Kipling, Rudyard	*Captains Courageous*
	Kim
Stevenson, Robert Louis	*Kidnapped*
	Treasure Island
Stoker, Bram	*Dracula*
Thackeray, William	*Vanity Fair: A Novel without a Hero*
Trollope, Anthony	*Dr. Thorn*
Wilde, Oscar	*The Importance of Being Ernest*
	The Picture of Dorian Gray

Victorian Literature
Writers Who Had Great Expectations

From my earliest days, I loved everything
about the sound, power and delivery of words.
                                        Phyllis Theroux

Genre: Victorian Literature
Shades of Charles Dickens
Task Five: Planning a Read-Aloud

You have read a novel from the Victorian Era. A characteristic of this period was reading a novel in a group setting, whether among family members or in public. Sometimes they read aloud, lifting the listener to a level of hearing the words of gifted writers. This invited the listener to hear the cadence, sound and beauty of language.

One writer who read aloud was Charles Dickens. He loved to perform and would give readings of his novels, both in England and in America. Once, when he left America after presenting his final reading, he called out to his thousands of well-wishers, echoing Tiny Tim, "God bless you, every one."

Now you have an opportunity to present a chapter from your novel to a family member or another adult. Here are some suggestions to consider:

- Preview the selection and practice reading it aloud.
- **Select a quiet place to read; avoid interruptions.**
- Be sure to set the scene and provide background information to help with the understanding of the selection read.
- Read with good expression and maintain eye contact.
- Adjust the pace in reading the story. **Don't read too fast.**
- Adapt your voice to fit the character.
- Use gestures, if appropriate.
- Ask a family member to read a portion of the selection. (Optional)

Upon completion of the read-aloud, you will ask a family member to write a brief assessment of your performance, including knowledge of the story, good expression and eye contact. A format will be provided.

Victorian Literature
Writers Who Had Great Expectations

'The time has come,' the walrus said
'To talk of many things:
Of shoes - and ships - and sealing wax -
Of cabbages - and kings -...'
Jabberwocky
Lewis Carroll

Genre: Victorian Literature
Task Six: Assessing the Portrait of a Reading
Adult and Student Responses

Having completed the Read Aloud assignment, write a description of your experience, using the format below:

Title of the Book:
Author:
Date of Reading:

Student Response:
Here you will write your description, including the name or names of the persons to whom you read and where and when you completed the task. Assess your performance. What needed more preparation and what worked well? Describe the reaction or reactions of the listeners. If appropriate, use dialogue.

The next part will be your family member's response or that of another adult. A signature is also required.

Response by a Family Member or Another Adult:

Signature from the Family Member or Another Adult:

_____

Teacher's Comments:

Assessment: Two grades will be given, one for content and one for mechanics.

Chapter 12

Poetry: The Golden Flax of Literature

Poetry
The Golden Flax of Literature

*I believe that the world is beautiful
and that poetry, like bread, is for everyone.
"Like You"
Roque Dalton
Translated by Jack Hirschman*

Genre: Poetry
Rationale for Teaching Poetry

Notes to the Teacher

Of What Value Is Poetry?

Poetry is an art form having dynamic, vibrant language. Drawing on the senses, poetry conveys memories, perceptions and feelings, all of which make it relevant and interesting. Writers of other genre bring us a perception of life, focusing on its experience. However, the poet communicates experiences imaginatively and creatively, deepening a greater awareness of the world. As teachers, we want students to know, respect and admire the substance of poetry and to understand and feel its power. We want to foster student interest, enthusiasm and passion for poetry -- even be dazzled by masterpieces.

Students need to learn the technical skills required of the poet and the process of writing poetry. Additionally, they need to see and understand how the poet utilizes devices such as metaphor, allusion, tone, repetition, rhythm, imagery, line breaks and sound, the most important. Sound includes such devices as rhyme, consonance, alliteration and onomatopoeia.

In presenting poetry, teachers might want to introduce and address preconceived notions students have about it, one of which is that poetry is "flowery" or that it is a means only to communicate feelings. This is not true! Poetry is important intellectually and should be a necessary part of any language study. Another stereotype is that poetry may appear to be more appropriate for girls than for boys. This attitude disregards the truth about poetry: great poetry is often written by men. Furthermore, poetry is not an easy art form. Reading and writing it is challenging and difficult and requires the poet to have a vast technical knowledge of language.

David McCord, a noted poet, has written, "No poet worth his salt has ever been able to write the kinds of poems he wanted to write without a basic knowledge of meter, rhythm, rhyme, and the established verse forms."

Another approach teachers may want to use in presenting poetry is to connect it to the lyrics of music, which is, in essence, also poetry. As you listen to a reading or responding to a nursery rhyme, an aria or an overture of a Verdi opera, a Beatle's recording or any contemporary vocalist's ballad, you have experienced the pleasures of poetry. Music and poetry evoke in us a response to their rhythmic patterns. Dylan Thomas describes his early experiences with poetry this way: "The sounds of the first poems I heard were to me as the notes of bells, the sound of musical instruments."

Writing poetry is hard! Good poetry, like all writing, is well crafted. Teachers should help students discover how precise poetry is written. The teacher's goal is to enable students to be comfortable in reading, discussing and writing poetry. The following suggestions are offered:

- Select poems that are relevant, meaningful, yet challenging.
- Provide poems that broaden the student's knowledge about technical poetic devices; e.g., figures of speech, rhyming schemes, alliteration.
- Ask open-ended probing questions to stimulate thinking and to validate students' opinions, recognizing that there are multiple interpretations of a poem. There is no right answer.

Helping students become excited about reading poetry will spark their imagination. The teacher must also ignite their creativity by having them write poetry, preferably in class. The pleasure of writing then becomes the best inspiration for writing well, coupled with encouragement and positive feedback from the teacher. The students' skills and sophistication in writing will improve through the reading and the influence of the works of poets.

Assessing poetry with a letter grade can be a sensitive issue because there can be a great difference of responses. Positive teacher input is of paramount importance and is encouraged. An effective way to respond to a student's poem include the following:

- Address and praise specific strengths of the poem.
- Question the student for clarification of the poem or any portion of it.
- Point out places for possible revision.
- Offer suggestions regarding word choice, imagery and form.

Assigning letter grades to student poetry may have an adverse effect. Students should recognize that the teacher is a "coach," responding to what works well in the poem and offering suggestions on how to improve it. If a teacher feels it necessary to assign a letter grade, it should be based on the completion and submission of a portfolio of a predetermined number of poems, not the content of the poems. The format for the portfolio is left to the discretion of the teacher.

Poetry
The Golden Flax of Literature

You will travel
in a land of marvels.
Jules Verne

Genre: Poetry
What Is Poetry?

Introduction

Poetry is an art form that pre-dates literacy as a means of recording oral history. According to the ancient Greeks, the word *poetry* means "I create" and evokes in the reader intense emotions of joy, sorrow, grief, anger, hate, beauty, love. One of the distinguishing characteristics of poetry is its economy and precise use of language, using predominantly specific nouns and vivid verbs. Samuel Taylor Coleridge believed that good prose consisted of "words in the best order," poetry of "the best words in the best order."

Moreover, poetry relies on sound, word associations and figurative language. It may also include sensory imagery: sight, sound, touch, taste and smell. Equally important, poetry has the ability to surprise the reader with an insight or further understanding of life.

Reading poetry requires the reader to be an active participant, to jump in and take part in the reading and writing process. The further you dive in, the more you learn. In the tasks that follow, you will be able to apply what you have learned and know about poetry and about writing it.

Introductory Activity to Poetry
Task One: Perceiving What Poetry Is?
Quick Write

To embark on your ". . . travel[s] in the land of marvels," you are now asked to write quickly for five to ten minutes on your perceptions and understandings of what poetry is and

- What it means to you. Consider the following questions:
- What do you already know about poetry?
- What childhood experiences, if any, introduced you to poetry?
- What was your reaction then? What is it now?
- Can you list some names of poets and their poems?
- Have you ever written a poem? Describe that experience.
- Is the study of poetry more or less or equally important as other subjects? Elaborate on your response.

Form a group of no more than four and select a recorder for this group. Each member will read his/her quick write and receive reactions from the group. The recorder will compile those responses to share with the rest of the class. Keep a copy of your quick write for inclusion in a poetry portfolio.

Poetry
The Golden Flax of Literature

*To hear. . . .children as they explore experiences -
everything being observed and responded to for the first time -
well, it's like the morning of the world.*

Lilian Moore

Genre: Poetry
Teacher-Directed Class Activity
Task Two: Becoming Familiar with Poetry

Notes to the Teacher

Select a poem from the list provided in this section or one of your own choosing that you think is understandable and meaningful to your students. Make copies to distribute to the class. Ask students to read the poem silently at least twice and to share with the rest of the class their ideas about its content and form.

Next, distribute to the students the list of "Literary Terms for Poetry" found in this chapter. Then, identify and discuss those terms that are evident in the poem, focusing on any three major devices or strategies. Discuss how the poet has shaped and spaced the poem.

Finally, distribute the list of poems also provided in this chapter. Instruct students to select a poem from the list or one of their own choosing and to secure a copy of it either from a book or on line. Have students bring a copy of their selected poem to class, striving to avoid duplicate choices. Schedule a few days to complete this task and the next activity.

Poetry
The Golden Flax of Literature

*And it was at that age . . . Poetry arrived
in search of me. I don't know, I don't know where
it came from, from winter or a river . . .
and it touched me.*

Pablo Neruda
Poetry

Genre: Poetry
Task Three: Reading and Responding to Poetry

In poetry, the poet invites you to dive in; and the more your eyes are open to the depth of the poem, the more you will see. There is always something new to discover in a poem.

Having selected your poem and with the list of Literary Terms, you are now ready to read and respond to your chosen poem. The following ways are offered as an approach to the reading and understanding of the poem. Make notations on the poem as you read for use in drafting a Free Write that follows:

- Read the title to predict the subject of the poem.
- Read the poem through a few times to get a sense of it, noting the punctuation as you read.
- Identify the validity of your predicted subject and determine the tone.
- Note the shape and spacing of the poem and jot down what you observe.
- Identify the speaker.
- Circle, highlight or jot down words in the poem that are meaningful or important to you.
- Highlight with a different color or jot down the poetic devices that the poet used in the poem.
- Look for repetition of words, imagery, sound and color.
- Identify the theme, if possible.

From your notes and focusing on both content and structure, quickly write your initial impressions and understandings of the poem and the poetic strategies the poet used to convey its content and form. Let your words spill out. Let each idea connect to another. letting each idea connect with another idea. Be sure to include the title of the poem and the name of the poet. Remember, there is no right answer; your ideas and perceptions are important and meaningful.

In a group of no more than four, share your poem and responses with the group. Members of the group are encouraged to give **specific** yet **positive** feedback of any kind. Each group will select one member's poem and response to share with the rest of the class. Additional **positive** comments and questions from the class are encouraged.

Assessment

Prepare a revised legible final copy of your quick write and a copy of the poem to include in your poetry portfolio. Include your original draft to have a record of the growth and development of your writing. The teacher will evaluate the completed portfolio at the end of the poetry unit.

Poetry
The Golden Flax of Literature

And as imagination bodies forth
The forms of things unknown, the poet's pen
Turns them to shapes, and gives to airy nothing
A local habitation and a name.

Theseus, Act V, Scene 1
A Midsummer Night's Dream
William Shakespeare

Genre: Poetry
Task Four: Reading and Writing Sonnets

Origin of the Sonnet

The sonnet originated in Italy in the 13th century. The word itself comes from the Italian word *sonetto*, meaning "little song." Sonnets are timeless, saying profound things about life and saying them artistically. They were meant to be read aloud. The English form, as we know it today, ultimately became known as the Shakespearean sonnet (c. 1609) because William Shakespeare used it with great mastery.

His 154 sonnets include a variety of themes, the most common being beauty, love, despair and morality. In addition, he included philosophical subjects and problematic ironies and made use of the *volta*. The *volta* is used in poems, particularly sonnets. It comes from the Italian word meaning "turn," also known as the "turning point." Signal words suggesting a *volta* include "but," "yet" or "and yet." A *volta* may be found in the third quatrain or in the ending couplet.

Shakespeare's sonnets have specific requirements:

* 14 lines written, with rare exceptions, in iambic pentameter.
* A definitive rhyme scheme and structure of abab/cdcd/efef/gg.
* Two quatrains that introduce the problem or ask a question.
* An additional quatrain that offers an unexpected sharp *volta* or "turn" and a solution to the problem.
* A couplet at the end that closes with a final answer to the problem or question.

Reading Sonnets in Class

Even though sonnets are intended to be read aloud, reading and studying them silently offers opportunities for reflection. The following Shakespearean sonnets have remained popular throughout the centuries. They are easily found in literature anthologies, poetry books and on line. Suggested questions for class discussion follow each sonnet:

Sonnet 17
"Who will believe my verse in time to come,
If it were fill'd with your most high deserts? . . ."

The theme of this sonnet is procreation. To whom is this sonnet addressed and what is the attitude? What is the advice? Where is the *volta*? What is the signal word or words?

Sonnet 18
"Shall I compare thee to a summer's day?
Thou art more lovely and more temperate: . . ."

The theme of this sonnet is love and its comparison to nature and human nature. Describe the poet's feelings about love. Where is the *volta*? What is the signal word or words?

Sonnet 29
"When in disgrace with fortune and men's eyes,
I all alone beweep my outcast state, . . . "

Sonnet 29's theme is gratitude. About what is he complaining? What makes him rethink his original attitude? Can you identify with the speaker of this sonnet? Where is the *volta*? What is the signal word or words?

Sonnet 91
"Some glory in their birth, some in their skill,
Some in their wealth, some in their body's
force; . . ."

The theme of this sonnet is values. About what is the speaker lamenting? With what life value does he conclude in the couplet? Where is the *volta*? What is the signal word or words?

Sonnet 130
"My mistress' eyes are nothing like the sun,
Coral is far more red than her lips' red; . . ."

Sonnet 130's theme is that the perception of beauty is subjective, or as many writers have expressed, "Beauty is in the eye of the beholder." Describe the writer's mistress. Why do you think the couplet is important in this sonnet? Where is the *volta*? What is the signal word or words?

Imitating Shakespeare
Writing a Collaborative Poem: a Sonnet

This part of this task requires the efforts of the entire class to compose a Shakespearean sonnet based upon what you have already learned. Be sure your sonnet has three quatrains and a couplet, all written in iambic pentameter.
Procedure
- Brainstorm ideas for possible subjects: friendship, nature, a sport, a specific viewpoint of your school year. The teacher will write the responses on the board.
- Select from the list of topics the chosen subject.
- Once selected, state the problem, conflict or question and possible solution.
- Compose the lines for the first quatrain as the teacher writes them on the board and state the problem. Be sure to use alternating end rhymes.
- Continue the identical process for the second quatrain.
- Decide where to place the *volta* or "turn," either in the third quatrain or in the couplet.

- Write the third quatrain.
- Write the couplet that answers the question or solves the problem or conflict.
- Read the sonnet in its entirety to assess how closely it conforms to the Shakespearean sonnet's format and structure.

Assessment

Students and teacher review and critique the process for writing a sonnet. Students then make a copy of the group sonnet to include in the portfolio.

Poetry
The Golden Flax of Literature

Poems should be like fireworks, packed carefully and artfully,
ready to explode with unpredictable effects.

Lilian Moore

Genre: Poetry
The Concrete Poem
Task Five: Playing with Words

Notes to the Teacher
Preparation for Task Five

Concrete poetry is also called shaped poetry, that is, poetry whose image represents the content of the poem and its literal meaning.

Select concrete poems to share with the students. Examples of concrete poems can be found in the public library or on line. The following sources contain examples of concrete poems:

Grandits, John. *Technically, It's Not My Fault: Concrete Poems.* New York: Clarion Books, 2004.
"technically, IT'S NOT MY FAULT."
"My Stupid Day"
"Mom Says, 'No New Pets!'"

Grandits, John. *Blue Lipstick: Concrete Poems.* New York: Clarion Books, 2007.
"Advanced English"
"Grown Ups Talking: A+, Grown Ups Listening: D-"
"Angels"
"The Bowling Party"

Janeczko, Paul B. compiled by, *Poetry from A to Z: A Guide for Young Writers.* New York: Simon & Schuster, 1994.
"Throwing My Weight" by Monica Kulling

Koch, Kenneth. *Rose, Where Did You Get That Red?: Teaching Great Poetry to Children.* New York: Knopf Doubleday Publishing Group, 1990.
"Heart Crown and Mirror" by Guillaume Apollinaire

Reading and Discussing the Concrete Poem

To help students understand the importance of the shape of a concrete poem and its connection with the content, the following procedure is offered:

- Select three to four poems to be read aloud in class **without the students' seeing the actual poem.**

- Read each poem and ask students to comment on the content and how it could be represented as a concrete poem.

- Distribute copies of each concrete poem read and compare the students' initial responses to the visual representation of the poem.

- Solicit student responses to both the content and shape of the poet's representation of the poem.

Once students have read, discussed and grasped what a concrete poem is, they are ready to compose their own poem.

Poetry
The Golden Flax of Literature

Poetry is like fish: if it is fresh, it is good; if it's stale, it's bad; and if you're not certain, try it on the cat.

Osbert Sitwell

Genre: Poetry
The Concrete Poem
Task Five: Playing with Words

For the Student
Background

The origin of concrete poetry can be traced to the ancient Greeks of the 2nd and 3rd centuries B.C. The Greek poets enhanced the meaning of their poetry by arranging letters and words in artistically visual ways. A modern famous example of concrete poetry can be found in the mouse's tail in Lewis Carroll's (1832-1898) *Alice in Wonderland*. The shape of the poem is a play on the word "tale/tail" as the words are written in the shape of a mouse's tail, progressing to a smaller size and ending in the point of the tail. Another modern famous example of a concrete poem can be found in the shapes of a heart, crown and mirror in Guillaume Apollinaire's (1880-1918) poem "Heart Crown and Mirror."

The term "concrete poem," as we know it today, emerged in the 1950s when a group of Brazilian poets defined the style as one that consists of its own structure. "In essence, works of concrete poetry are as much pieces of visual art made with words as they are poems. Were one to hear a piece of concrete poetry read aloud, a substantial amount of its effect would be lost," John Hollander points out in his collection *Types of Shapes*.

Based upon your study of concrete poetry, you are now ready to undertake the task of writing the initial draft of your poem in class. As a first step, brainstorm with your teacher possible subjects and shapes. The teacher will write your suggestions on the board or on a transparency. Next, follow the suggestions below to complete this task.

1. Choose a subject from the list or one of your own choosing. Think of a shape to represent it.
2. List 5-10 ideas or facts about the subject of your poem.
3. Outline lightly in pencil on paper the shape of the subject.
4. Write your poem on another sheet of paper. The length should be between 6-12 lines. Rhyming is not necessary.
5. Lightly, in pencil, write your poem into the pencil outline of the shape of the poem. If it doesn't fit, adjust the size of the writing or the size of the shape.
6. Erase the pencil outline of the shape, leaving the words of the poem, thus creating its image.
7. Write the final copy in class or at home. It may be handwritten or composed on a computer.
8. Read your poem aloud in a small group or to the entire class without showing the shape of the poem. Ask your classmates to comment on the content and how it might have been shaped.

9. Show your copy of the poem to the class. Solicit comments from the class.

Assessment

Prepare a revised legible copy of your concrete poem to include in your poetry portfolio. Include your original drafts to have a record of the growth and development of your writing. The teacher will evaluate the completed portfolio at the end of the poetry unit.

Poetry
The Golden Flax of Literature

*The real joy of poetry is
to experience this leaping inside a poem.*
Robert Bly

Genre: Poetry
Narrative Poetry
Task Six: Reading "The Fish" by Elizabeth Bishop

Biographical Sketch

Elizabeth Bishop (1911-1980) was born in Worcester, Massachusetts. She grew up in Nova Scotia, Canada, and attended Vassar College, earning a degree in 1934. Afterwards, she travelled to France, Spain, Ireland, Italy, North Africa and Brazil and, in doing so, she found inspiration for her poems. She wrote often regarding her love of travel in her poems, such as "Questions of Travel."

Settling in Florida, she based an early narrative and lyric poem titled "The Fish" on an actual incident that occurred there in 1938. With narration, imagery and tone, her observation of a fish turned into revelation.

During her lifetime, she was honored with numerous awards, including the Houghton Mifflin Poetry Prize Fellowship in 1945, the Pulitzer Prize for Poetry in 1956 and the National Book Award in 1970.

Class Discussion of the Poem
Note: The teacher will distribute copies of the poem obtained from an anthology, the library or on line.

Bishop's poem "The Fish" is filled with vivid verbs, rich imagery and abundant physical descriptions, allowing the reader to visualize the story as the poem unfolds. In writing the poem, she uses precise vocabulary associated with fishing and boat terminology, including the following:

swim bladder: a gas filled sac in bony fish that allows them to
  adjust to depth changes.
isinglass: thin sheets of mica, a crystallized mineral.
leader: piece of line used to attach a hook to the fish line.
bilge: stagnant water that collects at the bottom of a boat.
bailer: a device for draining water from a boat.
thwarts: seats for rowers of a boat.
gunnels: the top edges of the sides of a boat.

The students will first read the poem silently at their desks. The teacher will then read the poem aloud to the class, modeling appropriate phrasing and tone of the poem's content. As a result of silent and oral readings, the students will have gathered information regarding the poet's observations, descriptions and tone about the fish and the boat.

Bishop's narrative poem invites the reader to visualize the speaker's experience. The questions below are intended to guide you in interpreting the poem.

1. What are the physical and factual images of the fish?
2. What are the poet's reaction to the fish's situation?
3. What similes (direct comparisons using "like" or "as") does Bishop use in the poem?

4. What metaphors (comparison of two different things without using "like" or "as") does Bishop use in the poem?
5. Where are examples of alliteration (repetition of initial letter sounds, such as "b" or "s")?
6. Where are examples of rhythm found in the poem?
7. What marks the crucial point in the poem, resulting in the speaker's change in attitude toward the fish?
8. What does the image of the rainbow convey to you? Identify and explain the speaker's concluding message "rainbow, rainbow, rainbow!"
9. What inference can you draw from the fish's struggle for survival and the speaker's victories in life?
10. What revelation has this poem given you? Elaborate.

On Your Own
Writing a Narrative Poem

Poetry applies words to our experiences, to the situations in which we find ourselves. The poets we appreciate are important because they speak for us and teach us to speak for ourselves. In essence, they are role models. Elizabeth Bishop's lyric poem successfully accomplished and surpassed Robert Frost's description of poetry when he said, "Poetry is when an emotion has found its thought and the thought has found words."

Bishop based her poem on an incident that occurred in her life. The tone is factual, unsentimental, insightful and, at times, sympathetic. The poem ends with an element of surprise.

You now have the opportunity to write your own narrative poem. Begin with your own experiences and perceptions. Brainstorm on a sheet of paper ideas for your subject. It can be an incident that happened to you, to your family members or to your friend. It can be a memory that haunts you, a startling dream, an exciting adventure or a deeply personal situation. Think of what you are doing as an exploration.

Once you have decided on your subject, start writing for at least ten minutes. Include factual descriptions and personal reality. Use vivid verbs and specific nouns to create an image in the reader's mind. As you write, keep rereading your poem to gain a sense of its rhythm and word sound. Try to end your poem with an element of surprise or significance.

The Writing Process

After writing the first draft of your poem, the next step is its revision. Revision means re-seeing your poem, considering matters of content and form. Revision requires making linguistic and organizational choices that include adding, subtracting, reordering and substituting words. Be sure your poem brings out the narrative's details and paints images for the reader. You may want to include color in your poem and/or repeat key words or phrases.

Another step in the writing process is editing, which necessitates correcting mistakes in punctuation, spelling and vocabulary so that your final draft conforms to the rules of Standard English.

The final step of the writing process involves careful proofreading of your entire poem, correcting any additional errors.

Remember, the title for the poem comes from the content and should be decided at the end.

Summing Up: A Poetry Reading

In groups of four or five, read and discuss your poem. Ask the members to focus on what works well in your poem and areas for **possible** revision. Remember, you as the author have the final choice. Each group will select a poem to be read to the class.

Assessment

Prepare a revised legible copy of your narrative poem to include in your poetry portfolio. Include your original drafts to have a record of the growth and development of your writing. The teacher will evaluate the completed portfolio at the end of the poetry unit.

Literary Terms for Poetry

ALLITERATION: the repetition of initial consonant sounds to draw attention to certain words or ideas.

ALLUSION: a reference to a well-known place, person, literary work or work of art.

ASSONANCE: the repetition of internal vowel sounds.

BALLAD: a narrative poem or song derived from oral tradition.

BLANK VERSE: iambic pentameter without end rhyme.

CADENCE: the rhythmic flow of poetry.

COLLABORATIVE POEM: a poem written by two or more people.

CONCRETE POEM: a poem with a shape or image that represents its subject.

CONSONANCE: the repetition of consonant sounds within or at the end of words.

COUPLET: a two-line stanza with end rhyme.

FIGURATIVE LANGUAGE: writing that is not meant to be taken literally. The common examples include the following:
- **Hyperbole:** exaggeration or overstatement for dramatic effect.
- **Metaphor:** a comparison between two unlike things, without the use of **"like"** or **"as."**
- **Simile:** a figure of speech that makes an explicit comparison between two unlike things and uses **"like "**or **"as"** to show the comparison.
- **Personification:** figurative language in which an object, animal or idea is given human characteristics.

FREE VERSE: poetry that does not have regular patterns of rhythm and meter.

IAMB: a metrical foot consisting of an unaccented syllable followed by an accented one.

IMAGE: a word or phrase that appeals to one or more of the five senses: sight, sound, touch, taste or smell.

LINE BREAKS: the place where a poet ends one line and begins another.

LYRIC POETRY: short non-narrative poetry that expresses strong emotion.

METER: the rhythmical pattern of a poem, determined by the number of stresses or beats, in each line.

NARRATIVE POETRY: poetry that tells a story.

ODE: a poem about a person, an object or animal.

ONOMATOPOEIA: the use of words that imitate sounds, such as *crash, screech, hiss, bang, jingle.*

POETRY: a term applied to stanzas in which poets express their perceptions of the world.

QUATRAIN: a four-line stanza of poetry.

RHYME: repetition of sounds that rhyme with the same sound, either in the middle or end of lines.

RHYTHM: the arrangement of stressed and unstressed syllables in a poem.

SCANSION: the counting of poetic feet and its analysis to determine the meter.

SONNET: the two types of sonnets are Petrarchan and Shakespearean, also known as the Italian and English sonnet. Both include poems with fourteen lines and written in iambic pentameter. The Shakespearean sonnet has three quatrains   followed by a rhymed couplet with the rhyme scheme abab/cdcd/efef/gg.

SPEAKER: the narrator's voice in a poem, which may be that of the poet or a fictional character.

STANZA: a group of lines in a poem that functions like paragraphs in prose.

SYMBOL: a person, place or thing that represents something else.

TONE: the voice of the speaker in the poem expressing the speaker's attitude toward the subject.

VERSE: a unit in poetry.

VILLANELLE: a form of poetry with six stanzas, consisting of five tercets, a final quatrain and the rhyme scheme aba/aba/aba/aba/aba/abba.

VOLTA: an Italian term meaning "turn" or "turning point" in a literary work, but mainly found in sonnets.

Voices of the Poets

*Read the poems that touch the heart, disturb
the intelligence, and lodge in the memory.*
J.D. McClatchy

Many of the poems cited below can easily be found in literature anthologies or on line. The list includes poets from ancient China to the Renaissance and more contemporary poets of the 21st century.

Allen, Samuel	To Satch
Ambler, Andrea L.	Light Comes In (Royal Fireworks)
	Going Home (Royal Fireworks)
Ambler, Andrea & Hal	Le Jardin de Therese (Royal Fireworks)
Amichai, Yehuda	Oath Of Friendship
Apollinaire, Guillaume	Heart Crown and Mirror
Browning, Elizabeth Barrett	The Best
	Sonnet 14
Bishop, Elizabeth	One Art
Blake, William	A Poison Tree
	To see a World…
Bly, Robert	Driving to Town Late to Mail a Letter
Booth, Phillip	First Lesson
Cane, Melville	Snow Toward Evening
Cardiff, Gladys	Combing
Cedering, Siv	Suppose
Charles, Dorthi	Concrete Cat
Ciardi, John	A Lesson in Manners
Cornford, Frances	Childhood
Corpi, Lucha	Emily Dickinson
Crane, Stephen	Truth
Crooker, Barbara	Promise
Cummings, E.E.	Spring Is Like A Perhaps Hand
	next to of course god America i
Daniels, Jim	Speech Class (for Joe)
de la Mare, Walter	The Snowflake
Dickinson, Emily	This Is My Letter
	Some Keep The Sabbath Going To Church
	Bee! I'm Expecting You!
	After great pain a formal feeling comes
	As imperceptibly as grief XLV
Donne, John	Death Be Not Proud
	No Man Is an Island
Dove, Rita	Geometry
Elliot, T. S.	The Naming of Cats

A Selected Bibliography

Ambler, Andrea Louise and Joanna Vellone McKenzie. *Keepers of the Flame: A Poetry and Prose Resource Book for Teachers*. Unionville: Royal Fireworks Press, 2009.

Applebee, Arthur N. and Peter Elbow, et al., eds. *The Language of Literature: British Literature*. Evanston: McDougal Littell, 2002.

Boynton, Robert W. and Maynard Mack. *Introduction to the Poem*. Upper Montclair: Boynton/Cook Publishers, Inc., 1985.

Campbell, Oscar James. *The Sonnets, Songs and Poems of Shakespeare*. New York: Bantam Books, 1964.

Comley, Nancy R. "Poetry" in *Elements of Literature:* Third Edition. New York: Oxford University Press, 1982.

Farrell, Edmund J. and Ouida H. Clapp, et al., eds. *Arrangement in Literature*. Glenview: Scott, Foresman and Company, 1982.

Farrell, Edmund J. and Daniel Edythe, et al., eds. *COUNTERPOINT in Literature*. Glenview: Scott, Foresman and Company, 1976.

Fletcher, Ralph. *What a Writer Needs*. Portsmouth: Heinemann, 1993.

Gillan, Maria Mazziotti. *The Place I Call Home*. New York: NYQ Books, 2012.

Hayford, Harrison and Vincent P. Howard, eds. *Reader and Writer*. Second Edition. Boston: Houghton Mifflin Company, 1959.

Heard, Georgia. *Awakening the Heart: Exploring Poetry in Elementary and Middle School*. Portsmouth: Heinemann, 1999.

Janeczko, Paul B. *Reading Poetry In The Middle Grades*. Portsmouth: Heinemann, 2011.

Kearns, George, et al., eds. *Appreciating Literature* (Grade 11*)*. New York: MacMillan Publishing Company, 1984.

Kinsella, Kate, et al., eds. *Prentice Hall Literature: Timeless Voices, Timeless Themes*. Copper Level. Glenview: Prentice Hall, 2002.

Kinsella, Kate, et al., eds. *Prentice Hall Literature: Timeless Voices, Timeless Themes*. Bronze Level. Glenview: Prentice Hall, 2002.

Kitzhaber, Albert R., et al., eds. *Themes in Literature*. New York: Holt, Rinehart and Winston, Inc., 1974.

Koch, Kenneth and Kate Farrell. *Sleeping on the Wing: An Anthology of Modern Poetry with Essays on Reading and Writing*. New York: Vintage Books, 1982.

Koch, Kenneth and Kate Farrell. *Talking to the Sun: An Illustrated Anthology of Poems for Young People*. New York: The Metropolitan Museum of Art and Holt, Rinehart and Winston, 1985.

Koch, Kenneth. *Rose, where did you get that red? Teaching Great Poetry to Children.* New York: Vintage Books, A Division of Random House, 1974.

LeMole, G. Michael and Ray E. Willmuth, et al., eds. *Adventures for Readers,* Book Two. Orlando: Harcourt Brace Jovanovich, Publishers, 1989.

Lies, Betty Bonham. *The Poet's Pen: Writing Poetry with Middle and High School Students.* Englewood: Teacher Ideas Press, 1993.

Livingston, Myra Cohn. *Climb Into The Bell Tower: Essays on Poetry.* New York: Harper & Row, Publishers. 1990.

Marshall, Kristine E., et al., eds. *Elements of Literature: Sixth Course Literature of Britain with World Classics.* Austin: Holt, Rinehart and Winston, 1997.

Osborn, Patricia. *Poetry By Doing: New Approaches to Reading, Writing, and Appreciating Poetry.* Lincolnwood, Illinois: National Textbook Company, 1995.

Schneider, Elisabeth W., et al., *The Range of Literature: An Introduction to Prose and Verse.* New York: Van Nostrand Reinhold Company, 1967.

Thistle, Louise. *Dramatizing Classic Poetry for Middle and High School Students.* Lyme, New Hampshire: A Smith and Kraus Brook, 1999.

Historical Sites of American and British Authors

The National Steinbeck Center Museum, One Main Street, Salinas, CA 93901. Phone Number: 831-775-4721. Website: www.steinbeck.org. The museum is a tribute to the life and work of John Steinbeck. This interactive museum brings his stories to life and gives visitors a full sensory experience as they walk in the author's footsteps. A few blocks away at The Steinbeck House, docents serve up gracious prix fixe luncheons daily at the author's boyhood home. Reservations are required for lunch but browsing the gift shop is free.

Steinbeck Plaza at Cannery Row and Prescott Avenue in Monterey presents live music is often played at this historic site. The nearby **Spirit of Steinbeck Monterey Wax Museum** recreates scenes from California's past, including scenes from Steinbeck's novels. Open 9am-9pm daily.

The Museum of Edgar Allan Poe, 1914-16 East Main Street, Richmond, VA 23223. The Museum is said to contain "the world's finest Edgar Allan Poe collection." Called "America's Shakespeare," Edgar Allan Poe created or mastered the short story, detective fiction, science fiction, lyric poetry, and the horror story. The museum is open Tuesday through Sunday. Group tours are welcomed. To schedule a group tour, call (804) 648-5523 or email the Museum at jaime@poemuseum.org.

Emily Dickinson Museum, 280 Main Street, Amherst MA 01002. Phone: (413) 542-8161. The Emily Dickinson Museum is an historic house museum consisting of two houses: the Dickinson Homestead (also known as Emily Dickinson Home or Emily Dickinson House) and the Evergreens, built by the poet's father, Edward Dickinson, in 1856 as a wedding present for her brother Austin. The museum is open Wednesday through Monday, 10:00 a.m. to 5:00 p.m. Website: EmilyDickinsonMuseum.org. Email: info@EmilyDickinsonMuseum.org.

Mark Twain Boyhood Home and Museum, 120 North Main, Hannibal, Mo 63401 on the west bank of the Mississippi River. Phone: 573-221-9010. Website: marktwainmuseum.org. The Museum maintain 8 historic buildings, including the Boyhood Home, a National Historic Landmark. The museum is open year-round, 7 days a week.

The Mark Twain House and Museum, 351 Farmington Avenue, Hartford, Connecticut. Phone: (860) 247-0998. Website: www.marktwainhouse.org. The Mark Twain House & Museum, a National Historic Landmark in Hartford, Connecticut, was the home of America's greatest author, Samuel Clemens (a.k.a. Mark Twain) and his family from 1874 to 1891. It is also where Twain lived when he wrote his most important works, including *Adventures of Huckleberry Finn, The Adventures of Tom Sawyer, The Prince and The Pauper* and *A Connecticut Yankee in King Arthur's Court.* A stunning example of Picturesque Gothic architecture, the 25-room home features a dramatic grand hall, a lush glass conservatory, a grand library and the handsome billiard room where Twain wrote his famous books

Rowan Oak, the Home of William Faulkner, 2015 Rowan Oak, Oxford, MS. Website: www.rowanoak.com. Home to William Faulkner and his family for over 40 years, Rowan Oak was originally built in 1844 and stands on over 29 acres of land just south of the Square in Oxford, MS. The property & grounds at Rowan Oak are open year round, from dawn to dusk. While there's no fee to visit the grounds, there is a $5 cost for house admission. The property is maintained by the

164

University of Mississippi Museum and Historic Houses Department. Guided tours are available by appointment only. Call (662) 234-3284 to arrange for a guided tour.

Louisa May Alcott's Orchard House, 399 Lexington Road, P.O. Box 343, Concord, MA 01742. Phone: (978)369-4118. E-mail: info@louisamayalcott.org. Website: www.louisamayalcott.org. Orchard House is one of the oldest, most authentically-preserved historic house museums in America and brings the Alcott legacy in the fields of literature, art, education, philosophy and social justice to life. It is here that Louisa May Alcott wrote and set her beloved classic novel *Little Women*. It is called Orchard House because it contained 40 apple trees which Mr. Alcott considered to be the most perfect food.

Charles Dickens Museum, 48 Doughty Street, London, WC1N 2LX. Phone: 020 7405 2127. Email: info@dickensmuseum.com. Website: www.dickensmuseum.com. Visitors can see the house as it might have been when Dickens lived here. Rooms are decorated in the early Victorian style that Dickens would have favored, and personal possessions of Dickens from his lifetime as well as manuscripts, letters and portraits are on display.

Brontë Parsonage Museum, Church Street, Haworth, Keighley, West Yorkshire, BD22 8DR, United Kingdom. Email: bronte@bronte.org.uk. Phone: +44(0)1535 642323. The Brontë Parsonage Museum is maintained by the Brontë Society in honor of the Brontë sisters – Charlotte, Emily and Anne. It is popular with those seeking to find the source of the sisters' inspiration and is of particular interest as the Brontës spent most of their lives here and wrote their famous novels in these surroundings.

James Thurber House Museum and Thurber Center, 77 Jefferson Avenue, Columbus, OH 43215. Phone: (614) 464-1032. Website: www.thurberhouse.org. The museum encourages interaction, and visitors are invited to sit on the chairs, play a chord on the piano, and experience the museum as if they were the Thurber's guests.

Pearl S. Buck House & Historic Site, 520 Dublin Rd., Perkasie, PA 18944. Phone: (215) 249-0100. The Pearl S. Buck's birthplace preserves the home of the author and interprets her life from her humble origins in the Appalachian town of Hillsboro, West Virginia, to her rise to international recognition as a Nobel Prize winning author. The home is a cultural asset for the Hillsboro community, providing opportunities for education, recreation and economic development.

The Ernest Hemingway Home and Museum, 907 Whitehead St., Key West, FL 33040. Phone: (305) 294-1136. Website: www.hemingwayhome.com.Visitors can stroll through the tranquil studio, home, and gardens where Hemingway was motivated to write his novels during his most productive years. You will also see living there 40-50 legendary six-toed cats that are routinely cared for by local veterinarians. Some of the cats are descendants of one of Hemingway's cats, Snow White, which was a gift to him by a sea captain.

Helen Keller's Birthplace, Ivy Greens, 300 North Commons Street, West Tuscumbia, Alabama 35674. Phone: (256) 383-4066. Website: www.helenkellerbirthplace.org. Touring Ivy Greens will be spiritually uplifting as you touch the actual well-pump where Anne Sullivan reached into the dark silent world of young Helen Keller's mind and opened the window of communication. You will be touched too.

The Roald Dahl Museum and Story Centre, 81 to 83 High Street, Great Missenden, Buckinghamshire, HP16 0AL 01494 892192. Website: www.roalddahl.com/museum. The Museum, located 20 miles northwest of London, encourages children and adults to unlock their imaginations, engage with reading and have a go at creative writing. It is aimed at 6 to 12 year olds, features three interactive galleries. Boy gallery looks at Roald Dahl's school days while Solo gallery houses his original Writing Hut. The Story Centre puts your imagination center-stage with fantabulous activities to inspire the writer in you.

Harriet Beecher Stowe House and Center, 77 Forest Street Hartford, CT 06105. Phone: (860) 522-9258. Website: www.harrietbeecherstowecenter.org. Most of the furnishings in the house belonged to Stowe or members of her family, and the interior incorporates her preference for informal homemaking. The furnishings are a blend of 18th century family heirlooms alongside Empire and Victorian pieces. Family photographs stand near Stowe's souvenir copies of Raphael's *Madonna of the Goldfinch* and the *Venus de Milo*. Stowe's own oils and watercolors attest to her artistic talent. The exterior paint reproduces colors Stowe chose in 1878 and the grounds illustrate her fondness for gardening.